Praise for *Mediactive*

"Dan Gillmor has thought more deeply, more usefully, and over a longer period of time about the next stages of media evolution than just about anyone else. In *Mediactive*, he puts the results of his ideas and experiments together in a guide full of practical tips and longer-term inspirations for everyone affected by rapid changes in the news ecology. This book is a very worthy successor to his influential *We the Media*."

--James Fallows, *Atlantic Magazine,* author of *Postcards from Tomorrow Square* and *Breaking the News*

"Dan's book helps us understand when the news we read is reliable and trustworthy, and how to determine when what we're reading is intended to deceive. A trustworthy press is required for the survival of a democracy, and we really need this book right now."

--Craig Newmark, founder of craigslist

"A master-class in media-literacy for the 21st century, operating on all scales from the tiniest details of navigating wiki software all the way up to sensible and smart suggestions for reforming law and policy to make the news better and fairer. Gillmor's a reporter's reporter for the information age, *Mediactive* made me want to stand up and salute."

--Cory Doctorow, co-editor/owner, Boing Boing; author of *For the Win*

"As the lines between professional and citizen journalists continue to blur, *Mediactive* provides a useful roadmap to help us become savvier consumers and creators alike."

-- Steve Case, chairman and CEO of Revolution and co-founder of America Online

"It's all true – at least to someone. And that's the problem in a hypermediated world where everyone and anyone can represent his own reality. Gillmor attacks the problem of representation and reality head on, demanding we become media-active users of our emerging media, instead of passive consumers. If this book doesn't get you out of Facebook and back on the real Internet, nothing will."

--Douglas Rushkoff, author of *Program or Be Programmed: Ten Commands for a Digital Age*

"An important book showing people how to swim rather than drown in today's torrent of information. Dan Gillmor lives on the front line of digital information – there's no-one better to help us understand the risks and opportunities or help us ask the right questions."

--Richard Sambrook, Global Vice Chairman and Chief Content Officer at Edelman, and former BBC Director of Global News

"With the future of journalism and democracy in peril, *Mediactive* comes along with sage and practical advice at a crucial time. Dan Gillmor, pioneering journalist and teacher of journalists, offers a practical guide to citizens who now need to become active producers as well as critical consumers of media. Read this book right away, buy one for a friend and another one for a student, and then put Gillmor's advice into action."

--Howard Rheingold, author of the *Smart Mobs* and other books about our digital future

"Dan Gillmor's first book, *We the Media*, was an indispensible guide to the rise of the "former audience" — that is, to the vital role that consumers of media were beginning to play in creating and distributing media. Now, in *Mediactive*, Gillmor builds on his earlier work by explaining clearly and concisely how to achieve media literacy in the digital age. Through common-sense guidelines and well-chosen examples, Gillmor shows how anyone can navigate the half-truths, exaggerations and outright falsehoods that permeate today's media environment and ferret out what is true and important. As Gillmor writes, 'When we have unlimited sources of information, and when so much of what comes at us is questionable, our lives get more challenging. They also get more interesting.'"

--Dan Kennedy, assistant professor of journalism at Northeastern University, former Boston Phoenix media critic, and author of the Media Nation blog at www.dankennedy.net

Mediactive

Mediactive

By Dan Gillmor

Contents

Foreword

As print and broadcast give way to the Digital Age, the media are in upheaval. The changes have sparked fascination, confusion and peril—especially when it comes to news, which is so essential in democracies.

We need a media environment that serves us, both as individuals and as a society. Yet turmoil in journalism threatens our ability oversee the people who act on our behalf. Media participation is critical to avoiding this threat: not just to keep politicians in check but also to balance the power of the whole crazy range of people we rely on—police and doctors and energy executives and pharmaceutical researchers and bankers, and all the other people who make decisions that affect us without requiring or allowing our direct input. Solid journalism helps keep those people working on our behalf (and it keeps us honest, when we work on behalf of others).

The turmoil is inspiring large numbers of ideas and experiments from people who know the risks and want to help create a valuable media in this new century. The experiments fascinate me as a writer on media and the Internet, and they fascinate my students at New York University and Harvard. They differ in small and large ways, but most have at least one thing in common: They imagine trying to fix the supply of news, either by vetting or filtering sources in such a way as to preserve the old, relatively passive grazing habits of 20th century news consumers.

Dan Gillmor, as you will see in this book, takes a very different approach. Dan doesn't make upgrading the sources, or the gatekeepers, or the filters—or any other "them" in the media ecosystem—his only or even primary goal. Dan wants to upgrade *us*, so we can do our own part. He wants us to encourage media to supply better information by helping us learn to demand better information. And he wants us to participate as creators.

Dan's proposal for making news useful to us, as citizens and consumers, is the most ambitious one going. He wants us to become *mediactive*—active users of media—to help us live up to the ideal of literacy. Literacy, in any medium, means not just knowing how to read that medium, but also how to create in it, and to understand the difference between good and bad uses.

Dan's conception here is extraordinarily broad. Although he is a journalist, and is concerned with journalism and society, he conceives of media and our engagement with it across a broad range of behaviors, attitudes and tools we need to adopt. He offers a framework, first, for thinking of ourselves as active consumers, with the necessary virtues of skepticism and patience with complex stories, and with very practical guidelines for making judgments about the trustworthiness of stories and sources.

His framework then extends to us as producers, offering a simple but informative guide to many of the ways that we can now make our own media and put it out in public, advising each of us to participate on the network and also to have a home base online that we control. He offers advice on making the media we create visible to the people we want to see it (today, visible means findable). And in furthering his commitment to the "active" part of being mediactive, he offers suggestions on how each of us can be a trustworthy source of information, beyond simply vetting others for trustworthiness.

Dan's framework includes not just individual action but group action. As more and more of our information and opinions about the world are filtered through social networks, the book sets out ideas for being a good community participant, passing along not just links but context to one another—being as good at sharing and interpreting media for one another as we are for ourselves. And it takes group action to the highest order of aggregation: what kind of society we want to be, given our access to these new tools and to their attendant freedoms.

Dan has an extraordinary resume. He was the technology and business columnist for Silicon Valley's hometown paper, the *San Jose Mercury News*, both before and during the Internet boom. He was an early blogger, and one of the first to blog as part of his newspapering duties. He wrote a book on citizen media when almost no one had heard of the idea. He's run an academic program dedicated to treating journalism as an engaged and entrepreneurial field open to innovation, rather than a craft simply practiced by existing institutions. And he's been a participant in various media startups, as a founder, advisor and investor.

He's had, in other words, a ringside seat for some of the biggest tech-inflected changes in the journalism world, as an observer, a practitioner and a theorist. He knows what a revolution looks like, he knows the long odds against any revolution actually coming to fruition, and he knows when it's worth trying anyway, despite the long odds.

The obvious thing to say is that most plans this audacious usually fail. A less obvious but more important thing to say is that "most" is not the same as "all"; a few plans as big as Dan's do succeed.

The value in trying something like this isn't just the likelihood of success vs. failure, but that likelihood times the value created if we do indeed succeed. The possibility of making enough citizens mediactive to make journalism good because we demand that it be good, the possibility that a small but passionate group of both producers and users of journalism will become the people to do the work of holding society's powerful to account—well, that would be something of very great value indeed.

Of the current revolution, Dan says it's going to be messy, but also exciting. He knows what he's talking about. We would all do well to listen.

Clay Shirky (shirky.com) is a researcher, teacher and author whose latest book is Cognitive Surplus: Creativity and Generosity in a Connected Age.

A Note to Readers

In the pages that follow, you'll see that I've <u>underlined</u> many words and phrases. These signify hyperlinks in the online and e-book versions.

Since the entire book will be published online, this will enable you to quickly go to the Mediactive.com website and then on to the source material to which I've linked. I'm doing this instead of voluminous footnotes and endnotes, and for this project it feels like a better approach. (Not everything I know comes from the Internet, of course, and I've made clear in the text when I'm quoting from an interview or a non-online source.)

Why this technique? As you'll see, this project is not only the book you're holding. It very much includes the e-book versions and online material, and the latter, in particular, goes well beyond what's in the print edition. Think of this book as the easy-to-read, paper portion of the larger work.

You'll observe, meanwhile, that there's no index. That's also deliberate. Since the book will be online, all you have to do is a quick search. In the end, Google and other search engines are my indexes, anyway.

Finally, if you spot a mistake, let me know. Send me email at dan@mediactive.com. If I agree it's an error, I'll correct it online and in the next edition; and I'll list you as a valued friend of accuracy.

Introduction

It was one of those stories that grabs attention. The claim: A former U.S. Agriculture Department employee, an African-American named Shirley Sherrod, had misused her government position in racist ways. If you believed it when you first heard it, you had plenty of company—and you may also believe you have a plausible excuse. After all, you were told by Big Media, the Obama administration and the NAACP that it was true.

Except, as we've all learned since the initial media blast in July 2010, it wasn't true. It was a brazen lie, pushed initially by Andrew Breitbart, a right-wing blogger and self-described provocateur, and his allies at Fox News and other conservative outlets. Breitbart's blog post—which included a video snippet that gave an absolutely false impression of what Sherrod actually believed and had done—didn't spread only because of right-wing activities, however. It was given widespread credence thanks to the cravenness of many other media organizations, President Obama's secretary of agriculture and America's most prominent civil rights organization—a <u>collective fact-checking failure</u>.

I was lucky, in a way. I first heard about the story and Breitbart's role in it at the same time, so I instantly had doubts. I didn't doubt that an African-American could express racist ideas. What I doubted was that Breitbart could be taken at face value, based on <u>his record</u> of engaging in or assisting misrepresentations of his political adversaries' views and activities. From my perspective, that record constitutes evidence, beyond a reasonable suspicion, that the only smart way to approach his work is to wait for absolute proof—and not trust anything he says until seeing the proof.

Welcome to 21st century media. Welcome to the era of radically democratized and decentralized creation and distribution, where almost anyone can publish and find almost anything that others have published. Welcome to the age of information abundance.

And welcome to the age of information confusion: For many of us, that abundance feels more like a deluge, drowning us in a torrent of data, much of whose trustworthiness we can't easily judge. You're hardly alone if you don't know what you can trust anymore.

But we aren't helpless, either. In fact, we've never had more ways to sort out the good from the bad: A variety of tools and techniques are emerging from the same collision of technology and media that has created the confusion. And don't forget the most important tools of all—your brain and curiosity.

Many people who know me and <u>my work</u> may find what I just said ironic. After all, I've spent the past decade or more telling anyone who'd listen about the great promise of citizen media—democratized digital media tools and increasingly ubiquitous digital networks.

Make no mistake: I believe in the potential of citizen media more than ever, partly because I've seen some wonderful experiments that prove out the potential.

But the more thoughtful critics of citizen media aren't wrong about their main point: All information isn't equal, not in quality or reliability.

I care, as you probably do if you've picked up this book, about an undeniable reality: As media become more atomized, more and more unreliable information, or worse, makes its way into what we read, listen to and watch.

Still, I can't contain my growing excitement about the opportunities for participation that digital media have given us. I suspect you share some of that energy, too. Whether you realize it or not, you're almost certainly a media creator yourself to at least a tiny extent—and creative activity is intimately linked to the process of sorting out the good from the bad, the useful from the useless, the trustworthy from the untrustworthy.

Does this sound daunting? Relax. In reality, this is a much more natural and logical—and fun—process than you might be imagining.

At the risk of being too cute, I've mashed together two words—media and active—that describe my goal in this book, website and accompanying materials: I want to help you become *mediactive*.

At the very least, the payoff is that you'll be able to navigate the rapids, to better sort what you read (view, hear, etc.). If you're like most people, you've been mostly a passive consumer of media, and I want to help you to become comfortable as an active *user*. I want to help you minimize the chances that you'll get bamboozled, or worse, by the incorrect or misleading material that's all over the Internet (and, all too often, in what people call "mainstream media"), and to help you find trustworthy material instead.

When you become an active user of media, you can do much more than gain confidence that you know what you're talking about. Millions of people already are taking it further, engaging in the emergent global conversations that help us and our communities every day. You can dabble or go as deep as you want, giving flight to your own creative and collaborative instincts. The online culture is inherently participatory and collaborative, which makes this easy. And if you own a computer you almost certainly already have the tools, or free (or close to free) access to them. The advantages of using these tools are enormous.

Why participate in media, beyond becoming a more nuanced reader? Because your communities of geography and interest can benefit from what you know, and because being part of the deeper conversation can deliver so much satisfaction with so little effort.

Lots of new media conversations are entirely casual, or designed to provide nothing more than simple entertainment. But when we publish information we expect others to see and possibly use—whether it's text, video, points in a map or pretty much anything else—it's always best to do so in honorable ways that will engender trust in what we say. That trust has to be earned.

Please don't think of this as a chore. We're not talking about an "eat your (insert vegetable you loathe) because it's good for you" exercise. We are talking about doing something that's often fun or gratifying, and downright useful the rest of the time: useful for you, useful for all of us. But please consider this as well: In a participatory culture, none of us is fully literate unless we are creating, not just consuming.

And please, please don't imagine that I'm trying to turn you into a, gasp, "journalist"—a word that most people would *never* use to describe themselves, for lots of good reasons. I will try to persuade you, however, that if you want what you tell other people online to be trusted, it's worth following some bedrock journalistic principles.

There are infinite gradations of participation between sorting what you read more intelligently and being a journalist for pay; you can occupy any wavelength on that spectrum that you like at different times. Most of us will never be journalists, but any of us can—and many should—commit occasional acts of journalism, or at least contribute to what we might think of as our emerging ecosystem of knowledge and ideas.

Whether your goal is simply to sort through the information maze or to make your mark as a media creator, or anything in between, my goal in writing this book and establishing its companion website (mediactive.com) is to help. So consider what follows here as a "user's guide" to democratized media.

Although I'll offer lots of specific suggestions for being mediactive, the underlying message is more important: I hope to persuade folks to adopt some vital principles for being savvier consumers and creators alike.

We can expand our horizons. We can expand our knowledge. Time is the one thing we can't expand, but we can use it more effectively. Most fundamental is to rethink basic attitudes about media. That won't take any extra minutes or hours out of your day, and it will make the time you do devote to your media more productive.

***

This is an era of fast-to-market and even print-to-order production methods for physical books—that is, the versions publishers print on paper, bind between covers and ship to customers. These traditional books, which I love and still buy despite my digital habits, offer permanence and stability.

So, it makes sense to put in this bound volume the kind of material that doesn't change very quickly. While the tactics we might use to achieve a goal might vary from year to year, based on what tools are available, the principles don't change much, if at all.

Addressing the material that does evolve fast, including tools and techniques, makes much more sense on mediactive.com. For updates, especially, that's the place to turn.

I'm breaking the book into three main parts. The first defines the principles and explains some of the practices you should understand to be an active consumer/user—to get the best, most useful information so you can make good life and citizenship decisions.

The second part helps you extend that activity into the more hands-on sphere of joining the conversation in a more direct way. You'll find that being a media creator comes naturally (probably because you're already doing it in some ways), so the principles and practices of being a creator in a trustworthy way are also relevant here.

The final part ranges more broadly, exploring some issues important to our lives—and to our society—that we'll need to tackle collectively, not just as individuals. We'll also look a bit ahead, to talk about where we're going and what we need to get to the best possible mediactive future.

Part I

Darwin's Media: The ecosystem of media and journalism is evolving rapidly, growing vastly more diverse and confusing. How did this happen? What should we do about it? It's up to us, not just "them"—because we *are* the media.

Principles of Media Consumption: We start with principles because they are the foundation: Be Skeptical; Exercise Judgment; Open Your Mind; Keep Asking Questions; and Learn Media Techniques.

Tools and Tactics for an Active Consumer/User: Here, we look at some of the specific ways we can put the principles into practice.

Journalism's Evolving Ecosystem: It took a long time to get to where we are, and it'll take time to get where we're going. The ecosystem is becoming more diverse, and it will be more robust.

Part II

Principles of Media Creation: Be Thorough; Get It Right; Insist on Fairness; Think Independently; and Be Transparent.

Tools and Tactics for Trusted Creators: We'll look at tools for creating media, and techniques for becoming a trusted source of information.

Owning Your Online Presence: If you don't define yourself in this increasingly public world, there's a significant risk that others will define you. Moreover, you should create and maintain your own Web presence.

Entrepreneurs Will Save Journalism, and You Could Be One of Them: Experimentation is the rule now, and it's producing some great results; but traditional and new media organizations still have an opportunity to survive, if not thrive, in a mediactive world.

Part III

Law and Norms: The law applies in cyberspace, not just the physical world. Just as important, we all need to recognize that the law can't and shouldn't deal with some situations. Societal norms will need to evolve, too.

Teaching Mediactivity: Parents need to understand all this, for their own sake and their childrens'. Schools and teachers will also play a key role. We'll also look at why journalism educators, and journalists, should become leaders in this arena.

A Path to Tomorrow: What tools and techniques need to be invented, or perfected, so that we'll have the trusted information ecosystem we need?

Epilogue: How this book came to be an experiment in mediactivity, and how I hope it will change for the next version.

***

Who Is This For?

I don't really expect to persuade everyone to jump off the couch and become a mediactivist. That would be wonderful, but it's not going to happen.

If you are still sitting back in the cushions, though, maybe I can help you imagine the results of leaning forward and demanding something better than you're getting, so that you'll be better informed about the things that matter to you.

If you're already an active consumer, I hope to persuade you to take the next step and participate in the journalistic part of the mediasphere, even in a small way.

If you're a sometime participant, maybe I can persuade you to take an even more active role in your community's information flow.

We need one another's help. The rewards are going to be worth the effort.

Chapter 1

Darwin's Media

The email arrived in early January 2010 via a colleague, who got it from his father, who got it from a mail list. It began, "Do you remember 1987...."

The formatting and style were amateurish, and the tone just-folks. It went, in part:

> *Thought you might be interested in this forgotten bit of information.........*
>
> *It was 1987! At a lecture the other day they were playing an old news video of Lt. Col. Oliver North testifying at the Iran-Contra hearings during the Reagan Administration. There was Ollie in front of God and country getting the third degree, but what he said was stunning!*
>
> *He was being drilled by a senator, 'Did you not recently spend close to $60,000 for a home security system?'*
>
> *Ollie replied, 'Yes, I did, Sir.'*
>
> *The senator continued, trying to get a laugh out of the audience, 'Isn't that just a little excessive?'*
>
> *'No, sir,' continued Ollie.*
>
> *'No? And why not?' the senator asked.*
>
> *'Because the lives of my family and I were threatened, sir.'*
>
> *'Threatened? By whom?' the senator questioned.*
>
> *'By a terrorist, sir' Ollie answered.*
>
> *'Terrorist? What terrorist could possibly scare you that much?'*
>
> *'His name is Osama bin Laden, sir,' Ollie replied.*
>
> *At this point the senator tried to repeat the name, but couldn't pronounce it, which most people back then probably couldn't. A couple of people laughed at the attempt. Then the senator continued.*
>
> *'Why are you so afraid of this man?' the senator asked.*
>
> *'Because, sir, he is the most evil person alive that I know of,' Ollie answered.*

'And what do you recommend we do about him?' asked the senator.

'Well, sir, if it was up to me, I would recommend that an assassin team be formed to eliminate him and his men from the face of the earth.'

The senator disagreed with this approach, and that was all that was shown of the clip.

By the way, that senator was Al Gore!

Pretty alarming stuff, yes? Actually, no—because it's fiction, in service of outright propaganda. Oliver North never said any of this in any Senate hearing. Neither did Al Gore. (I know because, among other things, I checked with the Snopes website, where reality rules. I'll tell you more about Snopes in Chapter 3.)

What was going on here? It's simple, actually, as many of these kinds of emails tend to be. There were at least three plain goals: 1) Turn Oliver North, a right-wing icon of the 1980s, into a modern hero; 2) turn Al Gore, a born-again liberal, into a dunce; 3) use the fictional situation to promote the idea of preemptive military action and state-sponsored assassination. There's an honest case to be made for 3), but this email's fundamental dishonesty undermined that case for anyone who'd done the slightest homework.

My colleague had made it clear in his forward that he was skeptical. But how many people along the chain, before it reached his inbox and mine, had taken it for granted?

I don't have to tell you about the information mess, of which that email is just one tiny but toxic piece of flotsam. In an era of media overflow, we're swimming in the real and the unreal, and sometimes we wonder if we'll sink.

We won't—or at least, we don't have to. Sure, we find ourselves in a radically democratized and decentralized media culture that's producing an overload of information, an alarming amount of which is deceitful or just mistaken. But as we'll explore in upcoming chapters, this culture is also responding with important new tools and techniques for managing the flow and determining what's real and what's not.

Moreover, even as some people are spreading garbage, whether deliberately or inadvertently, others are giving us genuine hope for a future that's rich in trustworthy and timely information.

Consider, for example, the Ushahidi project and co-founder, Ory Okolloh, a Kenyan lawyer living in South Africa. In the wake of the horrific 2010 Haiti earthquake, Ushahidi—originally created to track election news in Kenya—launched an interactive "Crisis Map of Haiti" to track events in the shattered island nation. Information came in from people on the ground via SMS, the Web, email, radio, phone, Twitter, Facebook, live Internet streams and other reports. Volunteers at the Fletcher School of Diplomacy's "situation room" read the reports before mapping them, discarding items they considered unreliable.

Who was this for? Anyone who needed or wanted it, but the Ushahidi team hoped, in particular, that the humanitarian community would use the map as a guide. That's exactly what did happen. As a Marine Corps representative in Haiti texted to the organization, "I can not over-emphasize to you what Ushahidi has provided. Your site is saving lives every day."

Everywhere I turn these days I find people like Okolloh working to build and refine an information ecosystem we can use to make better decisions. Some are media creators. Others are helping us sort it all out. And many, like Okolloh, do a combination of both.

To make the most of what they're doing, each of us will need to recognize our opportunity—and then act on it. When we have unlimited sources of information, and when so much of what comes at us is questionable, our lives get more challenging. They also get more interesting.

Information overflow requires us to take an active approach to media, in part to manage the flood pouring over us each day, but also to make informed judgments about the significance of what we see. Being passive receivers of news and information, our custom through the late 20th century era of mass media, isn't adequate in the new century's Digital Age mediasphere, where information comes at us from almost everywhere, and from almost anyone.

That *anyone* can include you and me, and our neighbors and their neighbors. Somebody created that propaganda email about things Ollie North and Al Gore never said in the Iran-Contra hearings. Yet you, or I, or almost anyone we know, can create something as trustworthy as that piece of fiction was deceitful. That this door has opened to us is a powerfully positive and democratizing development. But anyone who steps through it needs to engage in a new kind of media literacy, based on key principles for both consumers and creators, which we'll delve into starting in the next chapter.

The time to work on this is right now. Our democratized 21st century media are a land of opportunity, and of peril. How we live, work and govern ourselves in a digital age depends in significant ways on how well we use those media.

The next two chapters will offer practical and effective ways to understand the digital media landscape and to apply that understanding in our daily lives. First, though, let's look back in time just a bit—some history will help us put today's world into context.

How Did We Get Here?

It has taken millennia for humanity to produce democratized media. When early humans started drawing on the walls of caves, they created a lasting record of things that mattered. Stationary cave walls gave way to rock and clay tablets, which in turn were supplanted by papyrus and animal-skin documents, including scrolls. Early books—single editions created by scribes—came next, setting the stage for what I think of as Media 1.0: the printing press.

Moveable type and the printing press, taking its early and most famous form as Gutenberg's Bible, liberated the word of God from the control of the priests. This was humanity's first profound democratization of media. Printing presses spread the words of individuals to many readers, in books, pamphlets, newspapers, magazines and more. Regimes shook, and some fell. Civilizations changed irrevocably.

When the telegraph first moved information over long distances at the speed of light, we'd hit a new turning point. Call it Media 1.5—the information moved from point to point but not directly to the people. This led to the next epochal shift.

Broadcasting is Media 2.0: mass media traveling long distances instantaneously. The radio brought news and information, plus the sound of the human voice, with an immediacy that led to the rise of both the great and the wicked. Franklin Roosevelt did much to calm a troubled nation with his fireside chats, while Hitler used radio, among other media, to pull his nation into outright savagery.

Television engaged eyes in addition to ears, adding the moving images of film to radio broadcasting's immediacy. It was a huge shift (Media 2.5), but not as great as what was to come.

The Internet is Media 3.0, combining all that has come before and extending it across the web of connections that includes everything from email to the World Wide Web. It is radically democratized media, in ways that we are only now beginning to understand well. But with this opening of what had been a mostly closed system, possibilities emerge, literally without limit.

And it's good thing, given what's happening to traditional media.

The Rise and Decline of Media Institutions

The same technology advances that have given us Media 3.0 have been near-catastrophic, at least in a financial sense, for what we now think of as the journalism industry—the collection of powerful corporate producers of journalism that emerged in the second half of the 20th century. Especially in the past decade, reality has collided—hard—with the news business. Publications and broadcasts are hollowed-out shells of their former selves.

What happened? The easy answer is that advertising disappeared. True, but too easy. Let's look a little more deeply.

The seeds were planted decades ago, when it became clear that newspapers and local television stations were becoming licenses to print money. The reason: The barrier to entry—the cost of presses and broadcast licenses, among other things potential competitors would need to enter those marketplaces—was too high. In the daily newspaper business competition was narrowing dramatically; by the latter part of the last century communities of any size with more than one newspaper were rare. So newspapers were monopolies, and local TV stations were oligopolies.

Monopoly meant charging ever-higher prices, not so much to subscribers, but to the advertisers who had nowhere else to turn in their communities if they had something they wanted to sell to the widest possible customer base. Nowhere were profit margins higher than in classified ads, those one- or two-line notices that filled page after page in most papers. In fact, for most newspapers classifieds provided the number one source of profits.

Wall Street loved the newspaper corporations, because monopolies are great fun for owners while they last; you can keep raising prices and no one can stop you. So when newspaper companies sold shares to the public, often to raise capital so they could buy up more papers, investors bid up the prices of the companies. The companies bought more and more papers: Profit margins kept soaring, and so did stock prices.

As Wall Street and private owners alike demanded higher returns, in many (if not most) markets monopoly newspaper managers became complacent and arrogant, to varying degrees—it's what monopolists tend to do. Rarely did managers care all that much about their communities; they were really just visiting on their way up the corporate ladders. The chief way they could please their bosses was to pull more profits from the local communities, by not just charging more for ad space, but also trimming back the budgets for journalism.

One thing they trimmed was journalism that aimed to serve people on the lower demographic rungs. Over time, most large daily papers increasingly aimed their coverage almost solely at the top 40 percent or so of the communities they served, in terms of household income—because those were the people the advertisers wanted to target. So newspapers were losing touch with their communities as they chased profits.

The Internet brought competition for the advertising dollars, as sites like eBay, Monster (jobs), craigslist and others gave advertisers a much lower price for a much better service. It didn't take long for the classified advertising business to melt, and with it the main source of profits at most papers. It will never come back.

Display advertising, meanwhile, was going through its own evolution. Newspapers depended mostly on big local merchants, notably department stores, for display ads. But economic forces led to consolidation of the retail marketplace—among other industries that tended to use newspaper ads heavily to reach consumers—and bang, another revenue source was gone for good.

Television's unwinding happened in different ways and at a different pace. TV is still a hugely popular medium and will remain so for decades to come, but the rise of cable and satellite gave viewers and advertisers more choices. These shifts were part of an upheaval for local TV, which at one time boasted profit margins that would make the greediest newspaper executive jealous. The effect of competition—and, I'm convinced, a relentless dumbing down of television journalism to the point that it was pure info-tainment—pushed audiences away.

And as all these financial storms were brewing, mass media audiences were joining advertisers in exploring the Internet's vast and diverse possibilities.

Democratized Information to the Rescue

The Internet didn't just take advertising away from print publishers and advertisers—it also brought democratized information to all of us. Actual competition for journalism, not just revenue, began appearing. And here, too, the industry has been ill-prepared.

As newspapers were coming apart at the seams, many traditional journalists began fretting that journalism itself was at risk. Who would do the journalism if the established business model died? How would the public be informed?

The anguish and hand-wringing, of course, raised a couple of questions.

First, by what standard had traditional journalists done such a sterling job that they were irreplaceable? To be sure, there had been some superb reporting over the years; the best journalism was as good as it had ever been. But some of our top reporters had helped lead America into a war started under false pretenses. And they'd almost entirely missed the building financial bubble that nearly ruined the nation. Newspapers increasingly focused on celebrity and gossip. They pretended to find two sides to every story, even when one side was an outright lie. Was this a craft that deserved our unreserved faith?

Second, did the unquestionably hard economic times for the journalists' employers mean that journalism itself would no longer exist if the employers disappeared? From my perspective, it seemed as though people working for traditional media companies were arguing that their enterprises had some near-divine right to exist. Not in the universe you and I inhabit!

I'm an optimist. I and others like me see renewal amid the destruction. We don't worry so much about the supply of news and opinion, though we do recognize that a shifting marketplace for information—from monopoly and oligopoly to a new, competitive mediasphere—will be messy.

Count on this: Tomorrow's media will be more diverse, by far, than today's. We can imagine, therefore, a journalism ecosystem that's a vital part of our expanded mediasphere and vastly healthier and more useful than the monocultural media of recent times—if we get it right. That *we* means all of us. Remember, Digital Age media are broadly distributed and participatory—broadly democratic.

For sure, we're headed for a time of abundance, at least in quantity. In that abundance we'll have plenty of quality, too, but it'll be more difficult to sort out. To assure a continued supply of quality information, we have to address the other side of a classic economic and social equation: demand for information that's reliable and trustworthy. That's up to you and me.

Trust and Reliability

In this emergent global conversation, as we ride a tsunami of information, what can we trust?

Trust and credibility issues are not new to the Digital Age. Journalists of the past have faced these questions again and again, and the Industrial Age rise of what people called "objective journalism"— allegedly unbiased reporting—clearly did not solve the problem.

We don't have to look back very far to note some egregious cases. The *New York Times*'s Jayson Blair saga, in which a young reporter spun interviews and other details from whole cloth, showed that even the best news organizations are vulnerable. The Washington press corps, with dismayingly few exceptions, served as a stenography pool for the government in the run-up to the Iraq War. And so on.

The credibility problem of traditional media goes much deeper. Almost everyone who has ever been the subject of a news story can point to small and sometimes large errors of fact or nuance, or to quotes that, while perhaps accurate, are presented out of their original context in ways that change their intended meaning. It's rarely deliberate; shallowness is a more common media failing than malice.

Having said that, I greatly appreciate what traditional news people give us in many cases: their best efforts in a deadline-driven craft. Despite the minor errors, the better media organizations get things pretty much right (except, of course, when they go horribly awry, as in missing the financial bubble until it was too late). The small mistakes undermine any notion of absolute trust, but I tend to have some faith that there's still something worthwhile about the overall effort.

Most traditional media organizations try to avoid the worst excesses of bad journalism through processes aimed both at preventing mistakes and, when they inevitably occur, setting the record straight. Yet too many practitioners are bizarrely reluctant to do so. As I write this, it has been more than a year since the *Washington Post* published an editorial based on an absolutely false premise, which I <u>documented</u> in my blog and passed along to the paper's ombudsman, who passed it along to the editorial page editor. The editorial page has neither corrected nor acknowledged the error, an outrageous failure of its journalistic responsibility.

I still don't know why the *Post* refuses to deal with this mistake, now compounded through inaction, but I do know that the silence betrays another major failing in the mass media: a lack of transparency from people who demand it of others. I'll discuss this at much greater length later. (On the subject of transparency, I should note that I have relationships, financial and otherwise, with some of the institutions and people I discuss or quote in this book. My online disclosure page, <u>dangillmor.com/about</u>, lists many such relationships, and I'll mention them in this book either directly or with appropriate links.)

One of the most serious failings of traditional journalism has been its reluctance to focus critical attention on a powerful player in our society: journalism itself. The Fourth Estate rarely gives itself the same scrutiny it sometimes applies to the other major institutions. (I say "sometimes" because, as we've seen in recent years, journalists' most ardent scrutiny has been aimed at celebrities, not the governments, businesses and other entities that have the most influence, often malignant, on our lives.)

A few small publications, notably the *Columbia Journalism Review*, have provided valuable coverage of the news business over the years. But these publications circulate mostly within the field and can look at only a sliver of the pie. As we'll see in upcoming chapters, the "Fifth Estate" of online media critics is helping to fill the gap.

The new media environment, however rich with potential for excellence, has more than a few reliability issues of its own. It's at least equally open to error, honest or otherwise, and persuasion morphs into manipulation more readily than ever. There's a difference between lack of transparency and deception, though. Some of the more worrisome examples of this fall in the political arena, but less-than-honorable media tactics span a wide spectrum of society's activities.

Consider just a few examples:

- Procter & Gamble and Walmart, among other major companies, have been caught compensating bloggers and social networkers for promoting the firms or their products without disclosing their corporate ties. This stealth marketing, a malignant form of what's known as "buzz marketing," caused mini-uproars in the blogging community, but a frequently asked question was whether these campaigns were, as most believe, just the tip of the iceberg of paid influence.

- Meanwhile, new media companies have created the blogging and social networking equivalents of the "advertorials" we find in newspapers, compensating people for blogging, Tweeting and the like and not always providing or requiring adequate disclosure. Federal regulators have been sufficiently alarmed by these and other practices that they've enacted regulations aimed at halting abuses; unfortunately, as we'll see later, the new rules could go to far if enforced too strictly.

- President Barack Obama has been the target of mostly shadowy, though sometime overt, rumors and outright lies. They range from the laughable to the truly slimy. What they have in common is that during the election campaign they were plainly designed to poison voters' attitudes in swing states. During Obama's presidency, they have been designed to discredit his authority among a large swath of the American people. The people behind these campaigns have succeeded to a degree that should scare every honest citizen. A nontrivial percentage of Americans believe Obama is a Muslim and originally a citizen of Kenya. If the latter were true, which it is not, Obama would be disqualified from holding his office.

- On blogs and many other sites where conversation among the audience is part of the mix, we often encounter sock puppets—people posting under pseudonyms instead of their real names, and either promoting their own work or denigrating their opponents, sometimes in the crudest ways. As with the buzz marketing, it's widely believed that the ones getting caught are a small percentage of the ones misusing these online forums. Sock puppetry predates the Internet and has never gone out of style in traditional media, but it's easier than ever to pull off online.

Craig Newmark, founder of the craigslist online advertising and community site, famously says that most people online are good and that a tiny percentage do the vast majority of the harm. This is undoubtedly correct. Yet as Craig, a friend, would be the first to say, knowing that doesn't solve the problem; it takes individual and community effort, too.

In a world with seemingly infinite sources of information, trust is harder to establish. But we can make a start by becoming better informed about what we read, hear and watch.

Innovation and Participation

Because we've become accustomed to a media world dominated by monopolies and oligopolies, we still tend to imagine that just a few big institutions will rise from the sad rubble of the 20th century journalism business. That's not happening—at least. not anytime soon. As I said earlier, we're heading into an incredibly messy but also wonderful period of innovation and experimentation that will combine technology and people who push ideas both stunning and outlandish into the world. The result will be a huge number of failures, but also a large number of successes.

One of the failures was mine. In 2005 I helped launch an experimental local Web journalism project called Bayosphere, and made just about every mistake in the entrepreneur's goof-kit. But since then I've also invested in several new media enterprises. I co-founded a site with a media component—users telling each other about where they were traveling, and giving advice on what to do once they got there—that worked well enough to be bought by a big company.*(I'm also involved

---

*My role in the second startup, Dopplr.com, was much less hands-on than my first one. I'm not sure if there's a correlation between the demise of the first and success of the second.

in several startups as an advisor, and serve as an advisor or board member on several media-related non-profits.)

I can't begin to list all of the great experiments I'm seeing right now. I'll explore many of them on the Mediactive website (mediactive.com), and mention at least a few in this book.

What's important is the breadth and depth of the innovations we're already seeing—even now, before the traditional media have disappeared or evolved. The experiments and startups range from not-for-profits doing investigative reporting to data-driven operations at the hyper-local level to aggregators of journalism from many sources, and include any number of other kinds of enterprises.

In one journalistic arena in particular, new media have pretty much replaced the old: the world of technology. The widening array of coverage, with some of the best focusing on narrow audiences and topic niches, has not only superseded the magazines and (shallow) newspaper coverage of old, but is deeper and fundamentally better. Some of this is exemplary journalism. Not all topics will lend themselves to this kind of transition, as we'll discuss later, but there's every reason to believe that many of today's weakly covered topics and issues will enjoy better journalism in the future.

I'm still having fun working on new media projects, but my money—literally, not just figuratively—is on a younger generation. For the past several years, while continuing to write and publish journalism online and in newspapers and magazines, including regular publication in the online magazine Salon.com, I've been working in academia. Currently I teach at Arizona State University's Walter Cronkite School of Journalism and Mass Communication, where I'm helping to bring entrepreneurship and the startup culture into the curriculum. We've encouraged students in a variety of programs, not just journalism, to team up and create new kinds of community-focused information products and services. Several have landed funding to take their ideas further, and all have shown the kind of potential that tells me we'll get this right in the end. I envy my students, and I tell them so; they and countless others like them around the world are inventing our media future, and the field is wide open for them in ways that I could not have imagined when I started my own career.

At the Knight Center for Digital Media Entrepreneurship, the ASU project we launched in 2008, my colleagues and I make this point to our students at the outset of every semester: There's almost no barrier to entry if you want to do something in digital media.

The tools for creating news and community information are increasingly in everyone's hands. The personal computer that I'm using to write this book comes equipped with media creation and editing tools of such depth that I can't begin to learn all their capabilities. The device I carry in my pocket boasts features such as Web browsing, email, video recording and playback, still-camera mode, audio recording, text messaging, GPS location sensing, compass headings and much more; oh, and it's a phone, too.

The other side of the media-democratization coin is access.

With traditional media, we produced something, usually manufacturing it, and then distributed it: We put it in delivery trucks or broadcast it to receivers.

With new media, we create things and make them available; people come and get them. Now, this isn't as simple as I've just made it sound. We get things in a variety of ways, such as RSS "feeds" and daily emails that come to us from many news sources; we also explore Webpages, Twitter tweets, Facebook messages, videos and so much more. Web publishers still look for ways to grow audiences. But I think of "distribution" in the new media world as the process of making sure that the people long known as consumers—that would be us—can find what's being created not only by commercial and institutional publishers, but by all of us.

Publishers and online service providers especially crave audiences whose members become active participants in a community. That's how some new media empires are made today: by helping the former audience become part of the process.

As media democratization turns people from mere consumers into potential creators, something else is happening. We are becoming collaborators, because so many of the new tools of creation are inherently collaborative. We have only begun to explore the meaning, much less the potential, of this reality. All I can say is, wow.

It's Up to Us, Not "Them"

In mid-to-late 2009, if you were paying even the slightest attention to the legislative debate over America's messed-up system of health care, you heard again and again about "death panels." These were the shadowy governmental bodies that opponents claimed would decide your fate if the Democratic-controlled Congress enacted just about any major shifts away from the current system. Tens of millions of Americans believed this, and many still do.

But if you were paying sufficiently close attention, you'll came to realize that the reports of death panels were not merely inaccurate; they were outrageous lies. They'd been concocted by opponents of pretty much anything the President might propose. (It should go without saying, but I'll say it anyway: Democrats have been known to lie to make political points, too—the Democrats' tendency to equate taxpayer-subsidized with "free" is an ongoing abuse of language and logic—but the death panel invention was especially egregious.)

The death panels lost their power in the public mind for several reasons. Most importantly, the charge was so inflammatory that some traditional media organizations did something unusual: They stopped simply quoting "both sides" of an issue that had a true side and a false side, and reported what was true. Of course, not all media organizations did this, and some continued to promote the falsehoods. But the issue was significant enough, and the consequences alarming enough if the charges had been true, that many people spent the extra time it took to figure out what they could trust. The public, by and large, learned the truth. And the health-care debate shed at least one flagrant deception.

We need to do this more often. We have no real choice.

When we have unlimited sources of information, and when the Big Media organizations relentlessly shed their credibility and resources in the face of economic and journalistic challenges, life gets more confusing. The days when we had the easy but misguided luxury of relying on Big Media are gone.

With new tools and old principles, we'll break away from the passive-consumption role to become active users of media: hands-on consumers and creators. This won't only be good for society, though it certainly will be. We'll be better off individually, too. The cliché "Information is power" is true for you and me only if we have trustworthy information.

Above all, hands-on mediactivity is satisfying, and often fun. By being mediactive, you'll get used to gauging the reliability of what you see, pushing deeper into various topics and following the many threads of arguments to reach your own conclusions—not on everything, of course, but on the issues that you care about the most. And when you've made that process part of your life, you'll have trouble waiting for the next break in your day so you can get back to to the satisfaction that it brings.

Chapter 2

Becoming an Active User: Principles

"What I like about April Fool's Day: One day a year we're asking whether news stories are true. It should be all 365."

The above quote is a Twitter "tweet" by Prentiss Riddle (@pzriddle) of Austin, Texas, posted on April 1, 2008. It's a line we should all live by.

Why don't we ask ourselves, every day, whether the news reports we're reading, listening to and watching are trustworthy? The fact that most of us don't is a vestige of the bygone era when we used to watch the late "Uncle" <u>Walter Cronkite</u>—called the most trusted person in America before he retired as *CBS Evening News*'s anchor in 1981—deliver the headlines. It's a vestige of a time when we simply sat back and consumed our media.

At the risk of repeating this too often, let me say again: We can no longer afford to be passive consumers. In this chapter, we'll look at the core principles for turning mere consumption into active learning.

Even those of us who spend a good deal of our time creating media, as I do, are still consumers as well. In fact, we are and always will be more consumers than creators.

Principles of Media Consumption

The principles presented in this chapter stem mostly from common sense; they involve the exercise of our inherent capacity for skepticism, judgment, free thinking, questioning and understanding. The tactics, tools and techniques we use to achieve this goals– blog commenting systems, for example—change with sometimes surprising speed, but these principles are fairly static. Essentially, they add up to something that we don't do enough of today: critical thinking.

The following sections look closely at the five principles of media consumption. Some of what this chapter covers may not be news to you, but in context it strikes me as worth saying. At the end of the chapter, I'll step back and consider the more philosophical question of how we can persuade ourselves to, as a smart media critic has written, "take a deep breath" as we read, watch and listen to the news. The next chapter will present some ways to apply these ideas to your daily media intake.

1. Be Skeptical

We can never take it for granted that what we read, see or hear from media sources of any kind is trustworthy. This caution applies to every scrap of news that comes our way, whether from traditional news organizations, blogs, online videos, Facebook updates or any other source.

The only rational approach, then, is skepticism. Businesses call the process of thoroughly checking out proposed deals *due diligence*, and it's a term that fits here, too. Let's bring due diligence to what we read, watch and hear.

I don't have to tell you that as their businesses have become less stable, the quality of traditional media organizations' content has been slipping. You've seen this for yourself, no doubt, if you still read your local newspaper. In theory, traditional journalism has procedures in place to avoid errors and wrong-headed coverage. But as discussed in the previous chapter, even the best journalists make factual mistakes— sometimes serious ones—and we don't always see the corrections.

Anyone who's been covered—that is, been the subject of a journalist's attention—knows that small flaws inevitably creep into even good journalists' work. And anyone sufficiently familiar with a complex topic or issue is likely to spot small, and sometimes large, mistakes in coverage of that topic. When small errors are endemic, as they've become in this era of hurry-up news, alert and rational people learn to have at least a small element of doubt about every assertion not backed up by unassailable evidence.

Matters are worse, and the audience response potentially more troubling, when journalists get big issues wrong. Most worrisome are errors of omission, where journalists fail to ask the hard but necessary questions of people in power. As noted earlier, the American press's near-unanimous bended-knee reporting during the run-up to the Iraq War was just one catastrophic recent example. Another was its apparent failure to notice the financial bubble that may still lead the world into a new Depression—in fact, some financial journalists were among the most ardent promoters of the practices that inflated the bubble.

Both failures demonstrated that all-too-common activity that constitutes much of modern reporting: stenography for the powers that be. The Washington press corps and financial journalists, in particular, have shown again and again that they crave access to the rich and powerful more than they care about the quality of their journalism. This is not entirely surprising, but it's no coincidence that the best journalism is often done, as in the case of the Knight-Ridder (now McClatchy) <u>Washington Bureau</u> between 2002 and 2006, by newspaper reporters and editors who have less access to the people in charge and spend more time asking real questions of the people who work for the people in charge.

The Two-Sides Fallacy

Another reason to be skeptical is modern journalism's equally unfortunate tendency of assigning apparently equal weight to opposing viewpoints when one is backed up by fact and the other is not, or when the "sides" are overwhelmingly mismatched. This is often called "providing balance" by journalists who are typically afraid that one side in a political debate will accuse them of being biased in favor of the other side. It is not "balanced," of course, to quote a supposition or a blatant lie next to a proven fact and treat them as having equal weight.

To use an admittedly extreme example, when you're doing a story about the Holocaust, you don't need to balance it by quoting a neo-Nazi. Nor is it "showing balance" to quote a climate-change denier in every story about global warming—not when scientists who study these issues have concluded with rare, near-universal fervor that climate change is not only real but presents an existential threat to civilization as we know it, if not to our species.

Nevertheless, in a mid-decade <u>study</u> the media researchers <u>Jules</u> and <u>Maxwell Boykoff</u> wrote that "53 percent of the articles gave roughly equal attention to the views that humans contribute to global warming and that climate change is exclusively the result of natural fluctuations" while "35 percent emphasized the role of humans while presenting both sides of the debate, which more accurately reflects scientific thinking about global warming."

Sometimes the dissemblers are genuine believers in what they say, even if they marshal non-factual evidence for their arguments. Worse are the paid liars: the people whose jobs involve the manufacture of fear, doubt and uncertainty about truth. The tobacco industry's long and infamous record of denying and obfuscating the dangers of its products is just one example of a case where deep pockets were enough to forestall, but not ultimately prevent, wider public understanding.

Paid to Persuade

Even more insidious are the deceptive people who are selling things or ideas but hiding their tracks. If you follow any major issue you're encountering them, though you may not know it. Sometimes they engage in what's called *astroturfing*, the creation of phony grassroots campaigns designed to persuade the public and public officials. Many deceptions originate in "think tanks" and lobbying firms paid by political and corporate interests—often their reports are widely quoted, generating commentary that often appears in newspapers and on TV, seeding blogs and comment threads, and generally trying to sell the products or ideas of the people paying them. I call this "opinion laundering." We'll never be able to stop it, in part because freedom of speech comes into play here, but at least we can try to spot it, as we'll discuss in the next chapter.

Whom do we trust? Sometimes, the wrong people. According to the public relations company Edelman's annual survey of trusted institutions, "people like me" are considered the most reliable, ranked above traditional media and other sources. This is a questionable attitude if taken too far. I trust a software-programmer friend to help me understand certain kinds of technology, but I don't have any idea whether he knows what he's talking about when it comes to wine or Middle East politics, and I factor that into our conversations.

The liars, dissemblers and opinion launderers are contemptible. But remember that they rely on credulous journalists who are too lazy or fearful to do their jobs properly. They also rely on us not asking questions ourselves. It's important to disappoint them.

Sidebar: The Apple Scare

In October 2008, someone using the pseudonym johntw posted an item to CNN's "iReport" site claiming that Steve Jobs, CEO of Apple, had suffered a major heart attack. This claim made its way to a financial blog and circulated quickly. Apple's shares tumbled briefly, recovering when it became clear that the posting was a hoax.

The incident led to something of a frenzy in financial and journalistic circles, including widespread condemnations of citizen journalism. In my own blog, I urged people to calm down. CNN got used. Maybe it was an innocent mistake. Quite possibly, however, this was the work of someone whose intention was to briefly torpedo the Apple share price. As of this writing, while it's clear what happened, we still don't know who did it or precisely why; I doubt we'll ever know.

This wasn't the first time false information had affected a company's market value. In the semi-famous Emulex case in 2000, for example, a profit-seeking fraudster who was trying to game share prices, posted false reports about the company to public-relations wires. He was caught and punished.

CNN's iReport had been running this kind of risk for some time. The labeling of the site has never been, in my view, sufficiently careful to warn readers that they should not take for granted that the postings by its semi-anonymous contributors are accurate—or that readers who make any kind of personal or financial decision based on what they see on the site are idiots. CNN did learn from the experience, though. Today, if you go to the site you're greeted with a pop-up saying, among other things: "So you know: iReport is the way people like you report the news. The stories in this section are not edited, fact-checked or screened before they post. Only ones marked 'CNN iReport' have been vetted by CNN."

Is that enough? It helps, but not every news-reporting outlet—traditional or new media—can be counted on to disclose such things, despite the fact that they all should. What does that suggest? We each bear our own responsibility to be skeptical, especially when we have little or no clarity about the source.

The fact that Apple's stock dropped, albeit briefly, was testament to the sellers' own stupidity. Yes, they were victims, in a sense, of fraud. And they had every right to be angry at the supposedly responsible financial bloggers who picked up the false report and repeated it (though the bloggers did qualify their reports by saying they didn't know whether the story was true). However, the sellers mostly had themselves to blame. They were fools not to take a second to consider the source, which was not CNN at all but a pseudonymous writer.

Investors fall into a special category as news consumers; they tend to operate on a hair trigger so they can profit from breaking news before other investors act and wipe out their advantage. As a result, they need to be particularly careful about where they get their information: The more they have at stake, the less they can afford to rush to judgment based on anything but trusted sources.

2. Exercise Judgment

It's not surprising that more and more of us are giving in to the temptation to be cynical. Institutions we once trusted have proven unworthy, in an era when greed and zealotry have prompted lies and manipulation to further personal and political goals, and when the people who should have been pushing back the hardest—including journalists— have failed us in so many ways.

Unfortunately, generalized cynicism feeds the problem. If we lazily assume that everyone is pushing lies rather than trying to figure out who's telling the truth and who isn't, we give the worst people even more leeway to make things worse for the rest of us.

That's why it's insane to generalize about our information sources, and why I want to tear out what's left of my hair when I hear Big Media advocates talking about "those bloggers" as if bloggers were all the same—or, for that matter, when I hear bloggers talking about "the evil MSM" (mainstream media) as if there were no differences among journalism organizations.

I'll discuss more in the next chapter some of the ways we can sort out what's true and what's false. The vital point here is that we have to give some level of trust to people who earn it. That doesn't mean we should turn over our brains to, say, the *New York Times* or *The Economist*, but it does mean that we should give them more credence than, say, the celebrity-driven tabloids that exist not to help us make good decisions, but rather to entertain us. Nor does it mean that we should rely entirely on what a single blogger, however talented, tells us about a narrow niche topic. It means exercising judgment.

According to danah boyd, a researcher at Microsoft (and friend) who's become perhaps the preeminent expert on young people and social media, our kids have embedded this thinking into pretty much all the media they use. They assume, she told me, that "somebody's trying to tell them a story and trying to manipulate them."

To an extent, I share this attitude. When I see a commercial product in a movie, I take it for granted that the company selling the product has paid the film production company to place that product in the movie. I think of it as an advertisement embedded in the entertainment, no more or less.

But if adults tend to separate news media from mainstream entertainment media, boyd says teens have a naturally media-critical sense that they're being given a story for some particular reason and they know people are making money off of it. "But it's not a level of in-depth media criticism," she says, "and so there's just this sort of—'Hmm, do I trust this? I trust my friends and what they tell me much more than I'll trust what these entities are telling me.'"

Is that good or bad, or something in between? boyd worries that young people, for all their skepticism, aren't thinking things through in a truly critical way:

> We don't live in an environment where teachers or parents or the people that are part of your adult world are actually helping you make sense of it and figure out how to be critically aware, but also to read between the lines to get something out of it. So as a result we end up throwing away the baby with the bathwater. Or we throw away all of it. We say—all of it must be irrelevant to us. When in fact there is a lot that is relevant. And this is where we need to get media literacy actually at a baseline into everyday conversations, where it's not saying that everything should be just consumed or rejected, but something where you consume critically.

We'll come back to this later, in a broader discussion of what has been called "media literacy." Clearly, we need to ask ourselves what kind of society our kids will inherit if they don't trust or believe anyone but their friends, regardless of whether those friends are well informed.

3. Open Your Mind

The "echo chamber" effect—our tendency as human beings to seek information that we're likely to agree with—is well known. To be well informed, we need to seek out and pay attention to sources of information that will offer new perspectives and challenge our own assumptions, rather than simply reinforcing our current beliefs. Thanks to the enormous amount of news and analysis available on the Internet, this is easier than ever before.

The easiest way to move outside your comfort zone is simply to range widely. If you're an American, read Global Voices Online, a project that aggregates blogging and other material from outside North America. If you are a white American, stop by The Root and other sites offering news and community resources for and by African Americans. Follow links in blogs you normally read, especially when they take you to sources with which the author disagrees.

Diversity can be a little harder to find in traditional media than online media, but there are numerous excellent publications focusing on different political points of view, different ethnic and national groups, and other types of differences. Spring for a subscription or pick up a recommended book on a topic you don't know about.

Whatever your world view, you can find educated, articulate people who see things differently based on the same general facts. Sometimes they'll have new facts that will persuade you that they're right; more often, no doubt, you'll hold to the view you started with, but perhaps with a more nuanced understanding of the matter.

Challenge Your Own Assumptions

Have you ever changed your mind about something? I hope so.

Evidence matters. One of the most serious critiques of today's media ecosystem is how it enables people to seek out only what they believe, and to stick with that. Television news programming is especially insidious. As Jon Garfunkel, thoughtful commentator on new media at his Civilities.net site and longtime commenter on my blog, notes:

> In October 2003, the Program of International Policy at the University of Maryland polled people about their perceptions of the Iraq war and corresponded it with the media they watched/read. The results aren't at all surprising:

> "Those who primarily watch Fox News are significantly more likely to have misperceptions, while those who primarily listen to NPR or watch PBS are significantly less likely."

Fox took the lead in featuring commentators with a particular ideological perspective; meanwhile, MSNBC has realigned its commentators so they have a mostly liberal world view. By all means, you should constantly be looking for evidence to support your beliefs. However, it's also important to look for evidence that what you believe may not be true.

This means seeking out the people who will make your blood boil. Rush Limbaugh frequently infuriates me—not because of what he believes, but because he takes such enormous liberties with the truth and uses language that seems designed to inflame, not enlighten. Even so, I regularly read and listen to what Limbaugh and his allies say, because sometimes they make good points, and I can learn something useful.

Going outside your comfort zone has many benefits. One of the best is knowing that you can hold your own in a conversation with people who disagree with you. However, the real value is in being intellectually honest with yourself, through relentless curiosity and self-challenge. That's what learning is all about. You can't understand the world, or even a small part of it, if you don't stretch your mind.

4. Keep Asking Questions

This principle goes by many names: research, reporting, homework, etc. The more important you consider a topic, the more essential it becomes to follow up on media reports about it.

The Web has already sparked a revolution in commerce, as potential buyers of products and services discovered relatively easy ways to learn more before purchasing. No one with common sense buys a car today based solely on a single advertisement; we do research on the Web and in other media, making comparisons and arming ourselves for the ultimate confrontation with the dealer.

There's a lesson in this *caveat emptor* behavior. We generally recognize the folly of making any major decisions about our lives based on one thing we've read, heard or seen. But do we also recognize why we need to dig deeply to get the right answers about life and citizenship issues that are important to us? We need to keep investigating, sometimes in major ways but more often in small ones, to ensure that we make good choices.

The rise of the Internet has given us, for the first time in history, a relatively easy way to dig deeper into the topics we care about the most. We can ask questions, and we can get intelligent answers to these questions.

Investigation has limits, of course. No one expects you to travel to Afghanistan to double-check the reporting from the *New York Times* (though we should maintain a healthy sense of skepticism about what even such reputable sources tell us). However, there's no excuse for not checking further into the closer-to-home information that informs your daily life.

Near the end of the Cold War, President Reagan frequently used the expression "Trust but verify" in relation to his dealings with the Soviet Union. He didn't invent the saying, but it was appropriate for the times, and it's an equally rational approach to take when evaluating the media we use today.

5. Learn Media Techniques

In a media-saturated society, it's important to know how digital media work. For one thing, we are all becoming media creators to some degree, as we post on Facebook, write blogs, comment, upload photos and videos, and so much more. Moreover, solid communications skills are becoming critically important for social and economic participation—and we're not just talking about the reading and writing of the past.

Every journalism student I've taught has been required to create and operate a blog, because it is an ideal entry point into serious media creation. A blog can combine text, images, video and other formats, using a variety of "plug-in" tools, and it is by nature conversational. It is also a natively digital medium that adapts easily over time. Over a lifetime, most of us will pick up many kinds of newer media forms, or readapt older ones; a personal blog, for example, is a lot like an old-fashioned diary, with the major exception that most blogs are intended to be public.

Media-creation skills are becoming part of the educational process for many children in the developed world (less so for other children). In the U.S. and other economically advanced nations, teenagers and younger children are what some call "digital natives," though some of the most savvy users of digital technology are older people who have learned how to use it and who bring other, crucial skills—most notably critical thinking and an appreciation of nuance—to the table.

Young or old, learning how to snap a photo with a mobile phone is useful, but it's just as important to know all the possibilities of what you can do with that picture and to understand how it fits into a larger media ecosystem.

Also, it's essential to grasp the ways people use media to persuade and manipulate—that is, how media creators push our logical and emotional buttons. Understanding this also means knowing how to distinguish a marketer from a journalist, and a non-journalistic blogger from one whose work does serve a journalistic purpose; all create media, but they have different goals.

All this is part of the broader grasp of how journalism works. The craft and business are evolving, but they still exert an enormous influence over the way people live. In one sense, some journalists are an example of a second-order effect of the marketers' trade, because sellers and persuaders do all they can to use journalists to amplify their messages.

Happily, as the mediasphere becomes ever more diverse, it is unleashing forces that ensure greater scrutiny of journalism. This helps us become more mediactive.

Media criticism was a somewhat sleepy field until bloggers came along, with only a few publications and scholarly journals serving as the only serious watchdogs of a press that had become complacent and arrogant. Journalists themselves rarely covered each other, except in the way they covered celebrities of all kinds. This wasn't a conspiracy of silence, but it was taken as given that only the most egregious behavior (or undeniable triumphs) were worthy of note in competitive journals or broadcasts.

Thankfully, bloggers, in particular, have become ardent examples of the new breed of media critics. Some are small-time jerks, dogs chasing cars because it's their instinct to do so. But many are the real thing: serious, impassioned critics who deserve respect for performing the watchdog role so important to the rest of us.

We all need to help each other sort out the information we can trust from that we shouldn't. This will be complicated, but if we get it right, the value will be immeasurable.

Toward a Slower News Culture

On Nov. 5, 2009, in the minutes and hours after an Army officer opened fire on his fellow soldiers at Fort Hood, Texas, the media floodgates opened in the now-standard way. A torrent of news reports and commentary poured from the scene, the immediate community and the Pentagon, amplified by corollary data, informed commentary and rank speculation from journalists, bloggers, podcasters, Tweeters, texters and more.

Also standard in this age of fast news was the quality of the early information: utterly unreliable and mostly wrong. The shooter was dead; no he wasn't. There were two accomplices; no there weren't. And so on.

Several critics tore into a soldier who was using Twitter, a service noted for rumors, to post about what she was seeing. Indeed, some of what the soldier posted turned out to be wrong. But was it fair to extrapolate this to brand all forms of citizen media as untrustworthy and voyeuristic?

There was plenty of wrong information going around that day, at all levels of media. Lots of people quoted President Obama's admonition to wait for the facts, but almost no one followed it. And almost no one heeded Army Gen. George William Casey Jr.'s advice the following Sunday not to jump to conclusions "based on little snippets of information that come out."

Greg Marx at the *Columbia Journalism Review* was among several commentators to catalog some of the misinformation that raced around. He wrote:

> It's not fair to lay too much of this confusion at the feet of [traditional media] reporters, who are mostly diligent and

conscientious, who are basing their claims in good faith on what they are hearing from their sources, and who are under tremendous competitive pressure to get the story first. But on a story like this, tendencies toward error, exaggeration, and inconsistency are built into the system, at least in the first days of reporting. In due time, a clearer picture will begin to emerge; in this case, we'll even hear from the shooter himself.

There will be plenty of time for analysis. Until then, let's all take a deep breath.

Like many other people who've been burned by believing too quickly, I've learned to put almost all of what journalists call "breaking news" into the category of gossip or, in the words of a scientist friend, "interesting if true." That is, even though I gobble up "the latest" from a variety of sources, the sooner after the actual event the information appears, the more I assume it's unreliable, if not false.

Still, I'm no different from everyone else in a key respect: When it comes to important (or sometimes trivial but interesting) breaking news, I, too, can react in almost Pavlovian ways from time to time, clicking the Refresh button on the browser again and again. I don't tend to immediately email my friends and family or tweet about unconfirmed reports, though, and if I do pass along interesting tidbits I always make it a point to add "if true" to the might-be-news.

What is it about breaking news that causes us to turn off our logical brains? Why do we turn on the TV or click-click-click Refresh or scan the Twitter feeds to get the very latest details—especially when we learn, again and again, that the early news is so frequently wrong?

Ethan Zuckerman, a friend and colleague at Harvard University's Berkman Center for Internet and Society, has some ideas:

- The media make us do it. [As noted below, I give a lot of credence to this one.]

- We're bored.

- Knowing the latest, even if it's wrong, helps build social capital in conversations.

- We're junkies for narrative, and we always hope that we'll get the fabled "rest of the story" by clicking one more time.

"I suspect there's some truth to each of those explanations, and I suspect that each is badly incomplete," Ethan says. "I also suspect that figuring out what drives our patterns of news consumption, and our susceptibility to fast, often-wrong news is critical" for having a sounder grasp of what we can trust.

Remember: Big breaking stories are literally exciting. They're often about death or the threat of death, or they otherwise create anxiety. Neurological research shows that the more of your personal bandwidth anxiety takes up, the less clearly you think. To get even more neurological: The amygdala takes over from the prefrontal cortex.

Slowing the News

A wonderful trend has emerged in the culinary world, called the "slow food movement"—a rebellion against fast food and all the ecological and nutritional damage it causes.

As Ethan suggested to me at a Berkman Center retreat in late 2009, we need a "slow news" equivalent. Slow news is all about taking a deep breath.

One of society's recently adopted clichés is the "24-hour news cycle"—a recognition that, for people who consume and create news via digital systems, the newspaper-a-day version of journalism has passed into history. Now, it's said, we get news every hour of every day, and media creators work tirelessly to fill those hours with new stuff. (Happily, a few newspapers and magazines do continue to provide actual perspective and nuance.)

That 24-hour news cycle itself needs further adjustment, though. Even an hourly news cycle is too long; in an era of live-TV police chases, Twitter and twitchy audiences, the latest can come at any minute. Call it the 1,440-minute news cycle.

Rapid-fire news is about speed, and being speedy serves two main purposes for the provider. The first is gratification of the desire to be first. Humans are competitive, and in journalism newsrooms, scoops are a coin of the realm.

The second imperative is attracting an audience. Being first draws a crowd, and crowds can be turned into influence, money, or both. Witness cable news channels' desperate hunt for "the latest" when big events are under way, even though the latest is so often the rankest garbage.

The urge to be first applies not just to those disseminating the raw information (which, remember, is often wrong) that's the basis for breaking news. It's also the case, for example, for the blogger who offers up the first sensible-sounding commentary that puts the "news" into perspective. The winners in the online commentary derby—which is just as competitive, though played for lower financial stakes—are the quick and deft writers who tell us what it all means. That they're often basing their perspectives on falsehoods and inaccuracies seems to matter less than that they're early to comment.

I'm not battling human nature. We all want to know what's going on, and the bigger the calamity is, the more we want to know—especially if it may affect us directly (if a hurricane is approaching, the latest news is not just interesting but potentially life-saving). Nothing is going to change that, and nothing should.

Nor is this a new phenomenon. Speculation has passed for journalism in all media eras. Every commercial plane crash, for example, is followed by days of brazen hypothesizing by so-called experts, but now we are fed their ideas at hourly (or briefer) intervals, rather than only on the evening news or in the daily paper—and even that frequency was too much. Only months of actual investigation by the real experts—and sometimes not even that—will reveal the real truth, but we are nevertheless subjected to endless new theories and rehashings of the "facts."

The New News Cycle

The advent of the 1,440-minute news cycle (or should we call it the 86,400-second news cycle?), which has fed our apparently insatiable appetite for something new to talk about, should literally give us pause. Again and again, we've seen that initial assumptions can be grossly untrustworthy.

Consider, for example, the Fort Hood shootings. We learned that the perpetrator wasn't killed during his rampage, contrary to what was initially reported. And that fact stayed with us because the story was still fresh enough, and the saturation coverage was ongoing, when reports emerged that he hadn't been shot dead by law enforcement.

However, we all also "know" false things that were inaccurately reported and then later disproved, in part because journalists typically don't report final outcomes with the same passion and prominence that they report the initial news. We've all seen videos of dramatic arrests of people who were later acquitted, but still had their reputations shattered thanks to the inherent bias in crime reporting. And how many of us have heard a report that such-and-such product or behavior has been found to raise the risk of cancer, but never heard the follow-up that said the initial report was either inaccurate or misleading?

The abundance of wrong information in the rapid-fire news system has other causes than simple speed, including the decline of what's supposed to be a staple of journalism: fact checking before running with a story.

As Clay Shirky (who contributed this book's foreword) has observed—in a Twitter tweet, no less—"fact-checking is way down, and after-the-fact checking is way WAY up."

Clay's point lends weight to the argument for slow news; to the idea that we all might be wise to think before we react. That is what many of us failed to do during the early hours and days of the "#amazonfail" event of April 2009. As Clay described it afterwards:

> After an enormous number of books relating to lesbian, gay, bi-sexual, and transgendered (LGBT) themes lost their Amazon sales rank, and therefore their visibility in certain Amazon list and search functions, we participated in a public campaign, largely coordinated via the Twitter keyword #amazonfail (a form of labeling called a hashtag) because of a perceived injustice at the hands of that company, an injustice that didn't actually occur.

Like Clay, I came to believe that Amazon hadn't deliberately made a political decision to reduce the visibility of these books; it was, the company said (as part of an inept PR handling of the situation), a programming error. But I was one of the people who flamed Amazon (in which I own a small amount of stock) before I knew the full story. I hope I learned a lesson.

I rely in large part on gut instincts when I make big decisions, but my gut only gives me good advice when I've immersed myself in the facts about things that are important. This suggests not just being skeptical—the first of the principles I hope you'll embrace—but also waiting for persuasive evidence before deciding what's true and what's not.

It comes down to this: As news accelerates faster and faster, you should be slower to believe what you hear, and you should look harder for the coverage that pulls together the most facts with the most clarity about what's known and what's speculation. Wikipedia, that sometimes maligned mega-encyclopedia, can be a terrific place to start; more on that in the next chapter.

Can we persuade ourselves to take a deep breath, slow down and dig deeper as a normal part of our media use, and to deploy the other principles of media consumption to figure out what we can trust and what we can't? We can. And if we want to have any reason to trust what we read (hear, etc.), we'd better.

Chapter 3

Tools and Techniques for the Mediactive Consumer

Now that we've considered some principles, let's get practical and put those principles into practice. The key is going deeper into the news, leveraging your skepticism and curiosity and common sense toward that moment when you can say to yourself, "Ah, I get it."

What's involved? Mostly an adventurous spirit; remember, this is about exploration.

Among other things, you need to:

- Find trustworthy sources of information.

- Vet sources you don't already have reason to trust.

- Join the conversation(s).

As always in this book, what follows is far from comprehensive. Rather, it's a surface-level look at an almost infinitely wide and deep topic. Look for many more specifics and examples at the Mediactive website.

Finding the Good Stuff

At first glance, my daily media routine may sound time-consuming: I look at a few news-organization websites, including the home pages traditional enterprises such as the _New York Times_ and the _Wall Street Journal_, clicking through to articles of particular interest. I periodically glance at headlines in Google Reader and similar services, which collect links from a variety of sources, traditional and new, and are related to a variety of places and topics I've designated. I scan my email for items—articles, blog posts, videos, data and the like—that friends or colleagues might have flagged. I keep an eye on several Twitter lists, and I check to see what a few Facebook friends are discussing. If there's breaking news I care about, I check back with sites I consider authoritative or at least reliable.

Actually, all of that doesn't take too long. I used to spend more time reading a couple of newspapers each morning and watching the news in the evening. But I'm vastly better informed now.

I don't believe everything I read or hear, because I apply the principles in Chapter 2. And when I need to be absolutely sure about something, I dig deeper.

Given the relatively short time that we've been living in a digital-media world, it's common wisdom to say we're in the earliest days of figuring out how to sort through the flood of information that pours over us each day, hour, minute. But we already have many ways to be better informed.

I use a variety of tools and methods each day, applying the principles outlined in Chapter 2 through a variety of filters and tactics. But the main tools I use are my brain and my instincts.

The most essential filters are people and institutions I've come to trust. In the days of overwhelmingly dominant mass media, we had little option but to put some trust in those sources. We soon learned that they were deeply flawed institutions that, all too often, led us grossly astray or failed to address vital matters, global to local. But they also did, and continue to do (though less and less these days), some of the most important journalism. They'd have held more trust if they'd been less arrogant and more transparent. But there's real value, even now, in understanding what a bunch of journalists, including editors, believe is the most important news today in their own communities.

Aggregation—someone else's collection of items that you might find interesting—has become an absolutely essential filter. There's computer-assisted aggregation and human aggregation, in various combinations. Let's look at a few of them.

Google News, relentlessly machine-based, isn't bad as a zeitgeist of what journalists around the world believe is important (or was important in the past 24 hours or so), but Google's almost religious belief in the power of computer to displace humans has detracted from the service's usefulness.

Yahoo! once was the undisputed leader in aggregation, because it understood the value of human beings in this process better than others in its arena. It's still reasonably good, but it's slipping.

Topic-specific aggregation is rising in importance and quality. For example, I'm a fan of TechMeme for aggregating what's hot in the tech world, in part because Gabe Rivera, its founder, has clearly seen a vital role for human input in the form of an editor. (And while every media junkie has been reading the Romenesko blog for years, MediaGazer, a TechMeme site, is moving up fast as a must-follow service.)

Search has always been useful, but now it's vital. Google, Yahoo! and Bing offer useful news-search systems, letting you use keywords to flag stories of interest. When you settle on searches you find useful, you can scan the results for items you may want to check further. I search for things like digital media, entrepreneurship (which I teach) and many other topics that are of interest to me.

Bloggers are some of my best purely human aggregators. The ones with expertise in a particular domain, plus the energy to keep on top of the news, have become valuable brokers in my news consumption. If you're not following the work of bloggers who go deep into areas you care about, you can't be well informed, period.

Twitter has become a must-have alert system—but you should realize that it's the antithesis of slow news: a rapid-fire collection of ideas, thoughts and links, sometimes useful, sometimes not. The best "tweeters" keep up a flow of headlines—the 140-character limit on tweets doesn't allow for much more—that have links to deeper looks into what they're flagging. Probably the most exciting development in the Twitter ecosystem is precisely that: It's becoming an ecosystem in which others are creating tools to make it more useful. I'll talk more about how I publish using Twitter in an upcoming chapter.

If you follow more than a few Twitter-folk, you can easily get overwhelmed. My suggestion is to use the service's "lists" feature, which lets you create or follow—outside of your regular Twitter stream—different subgroups of people who pay attention to specific topics. I follow several lists created by other Twitter users, including Robert Scoble's "Tech News People," a list of 500 technology writers.

An essential tool for keeping track of everything we aggregate is RSS, or Really Simple Syndication. It's been around for more than a decade, and from my perspective only grows in value despite some suggestions that it's fading in importance. Essentially, RSS is a syndication method for online content, allowing readers of blogs and other kinds of sites to have their computers and other devices automatically retrieve the content they care about —and giving publishers an easy way to help readers retrieve it.

Those are only a few of the ways you can find reliable news and information, of course, and the tools, especially for aggregation, are still somewhat primitive, especially in aggregation. Later in this book I'll discuss the need for much better combinations of human and machine intelligence; for example, tools that can measure by subtler yardsticks than popularity will give us vastly better ways to understand what's happening in the world.

While we have ever more and better ways to find the "good stuff," as it were, there's a problem: We've also never had so many ways to find information that's useless, or worse.

What could be worse than useless? Information that's damaging if you act on it, that's what. So we're going to spend some time on how to avoid falling for things that are either wrong or come under the category we might call "dangerous if swallowed."

A Trust Meter

The first defense is our innate common sense. We all have developed an internal "BS meter" of sorts, largely based on education and experience, for dealing with many of the daily elements of life—including older kinds of media, from the traditional news world. We need to bring to digital media the same kinds of analysis we learned in a less complex time when there were only a few primary sources of information.

We know, for example, that the tabloid newspaper next to the checkout stand at the supermarket is suspect. We have come to learn that the tabloid's front-page headline about Barack Obama's alien love child via a Martian mate is almost certainly false, despite the fact that the publication sells millions of copies each week. We know that popularity in the traditional media world is not a proxy for quality.

When we venture outside the supermarket and pump some quarters into the vending machine that holds today's *New York Times* or *Wall Street Journal*, we have a different expectation. Although we know that not everything in the *Times* or *Journal* news pages is true, we have good reason to trust what they report far more than we mistrust it.

Online, any website can look as professional as any other (another obviously flawed metric for quality). And any person in a conversation can sound as authentic or authoritative as any other. This creates obvious challenges—and problems if people are too credulous.

Part of our development as human beings is the cultivation of a "BS meter"—an understanding of when we're seeing or hearing nonsense and when we're hearing the truth, or something that we have reason to credit as credible. We might call it, then, a "credibility scale" instead of a BS meter. Either way, I imagine it ranging, say, from plus 30 to minus 30, as in the figure below. Using that scale, a news article in the *New York Times* or *The Wall Street Journal* might start out in strongly positive territory, perhaps at 26 or 27 on the scale. (I can think of very few journalists who start at 30 on any topic.)

Credibility Scale

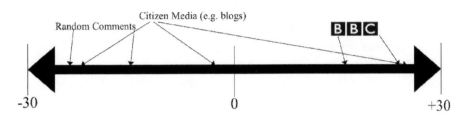

Now consider a credibility rating of zero. Sometimes I tell myself I have no reason to believe or disbelieve what I'm hearing, so I either discount it and move on, or resolve to check further. This says nothing about the material beyond an absence of information about and/or experience with the creator.

On my mental scale, it's entirely possible for someone to have negative credibility—sometimes deeply negative. For example, an anonymous comment on a random blog starts off in negative territory. If the comment is an anonymous attack on someone else, it's so far in the hole as to be essentially irredeemable—say, minus 26 or 27. Why on earth should we believe an attack by someone who's unwilling to stand behind his or her own words? In most cases, the answer is that we should not. The anonymous commenter—whether on a random blog or a traditional news site — would have to work hard even to achieve zero credibility, much less move into positive territory. (More on that below.)

Conversely, someone who uses his or her real name, and is verifiably that person, earns positive credibility from the start, though not as much as someone who's known to be an expert in a particular domain. A singular innovation at Amazon.com is the "Real Name" designation on reviews or books and other products; Amazon can verify the identity because it has the user's credit card information, a major advantage for that company.

Almost invariably, people who use their real names in these reviews are more credible than those who use pseudonyms. Not always, however: Andrew Breitbart did not hide when he "broke" the Shirley Sherrod story, as described in the Introduction. Still, his name was a warning signal to immediately put the story deep in negative territory on the credibility meter; the self-described provocateur's record for deception and inaccuracy was already well established. And the story turned out to be the reverse of the truth.

We can carry skepticism too far. Some people develop such deep distrust of some media that they reject all that they report and, conversely, believe whatever comes from media they see as offering the opposite view. For example, some on the political right reject anything the *New York Times* reports and uncritically believe anything offered by Fox News; and some on the political left reject anything reported in *The Weekly Standard* and uncritically believe anything they read at Daily Kos.

It's a mistake to give uncritical acceptance to any source—this can make people vulnerable to manipulation by untrustworthy people who appear to share their political perspectives. Many of the emails that bounce around the Internet—likely including the fiction about Oliver North and Al Gore, set in the Iran-Contra hearings, that opened Chapter 1—fall into this category, and they can come from the right or the left.

Checking It Out

In late 2009 a journalist in Tennessee wrote a shallow and ill-informed column (no longer available online) about citizen journalism, or rather what he imagined it to be. He discussed me and my work for several paragraphs and got almost everything wrong, including a) misspelling my name, b) misidentifying my current academic affiliation, c) claiming I'd left the news business when I stopped writing a column, and a number of other things. He capped this cavalcade of mistakes by advising everyone looking at citizen journalism to do what "real" journalist do: to check things out before believing them. I nominated him for the (nonexistent) Irony Hall of Fame (Media Wing). I got no reply to my email requesting corrections.*

The experience reminded me, not for the first time, that the news field would greatly improve if every journalist was the subject of this sort of poor journalism—there's nothing like being covered to understand how flawed the craft can be. It also highlighted two issues you need to consider when you want to gauge the quality of the information you're getting. One is simple accuracy; in this example, the misspelled name and wrong employer were egregious. The other is the choice of topic and the slant of the reporting; the Tennessee columnist wanted to promote his own craft while slamming something he considered inferior.

---

*I took the newspaper editor, Tom Bohs, to task at greater length on the Mediactive blog in a post entitled, "That Hallowed Standard of Accuracy: Oops."

Factual errors are part of the journalistic process. They happen, and in a deadline-driven craft we can understand why. But when errors are blatant and careless, they call into question everything else the journalist does. Worse, when they're not corrected promptly and forthrightly, is the message of arrogance they send to the audience.

Of course, you can't check everything out yourself. (Although you can and should, as I'll discuss later, be careful about what you create in your own media.) But when you're looking into something where being wrong will have consequences, and if you are unsure of the source of the information, you have every reason—even an obligation—to check further.

Howard Rheingold, an author and friend, has been at the forefront of understanding the digital revolution. In a terrific 2009 essay called "Crap Detection 101"(riffing off a long-ago line from Ernest Hemingway), he wrote about some of the ways to check things out. Here's a key quote:

> The first thing we all need to know about information online is how to detect crap, a technical term I use for information tainted by ignorance, inept communication, or deliberate deception. Learning to be a critical consumer of Web info is not rocket science. It's not even algebra. Becoming acquainted with the fundamentals of web credibility testing is easier than learning the multiplication tables. The hard part, as always, is the exercise of flabby think-for-yourself muscles.

Fortunately, crap detection tools are far more powerful today than they were a decade ago; the bad news is that too few people know about them. That has consequences: Many more people have started to rely on the Web for such vitally important forms of information as news, medical information, scholarly research and investment advice that the lack of general education in critical consumption of information found online is turning into a public danger.

So, no, Bill Gates won't send you $5 for forwarding this chain email. The medical advice you get in a chat room isn't necessarily better than what your doctor tells you, and the widow of the deceased African dictator is definitely not going to transfer millions of dollars to your bank account. That scurrilous rumor about the political candidate that never makes the mainstream media but circulates in emails and blog posts probably isn't true. The data you are pasting into your memo or term paper may well be totally fabricated.

There are innumerable tools and techniques that you can use to winnow out the falsehoods, and people who work hard to help you understand what's real and what isn't. Here are a few of my favorites. (As always, we'll be compiling a much longer list, broken out by topic area, at mediactive.com.)

Checking Out a Web Page

Howard Rheingold's Crap Detection instructions are a great place to start. Similarly, Scott Rosenberg (another author and friend) has come up with a long list of ways to check out a given website. A sampling:

- Does the site tell you who runs it—in an about page, or a footer, or anywhere else? Is someone taking responsibility for what's being published? If so, obviously you can begin this whole investigation again with that person or company's name, if you need to dig deeper.

- Check out the ads. Do they seem to be the main purpose of the site? Do they relate to the content or not?

- Look up the site in the Internet Archive. Did it used to be something else? How has it changed over the years? Did it once reveal information that it now hides?

- Look at the source code. Is there anything unusual or suspicious that you can see when you "view source"? (If you're not up to this, technically, ask a friend who is.)

Detecting Accuracy

Remember the bogus email in Chapter 1, where the writer was claiming things about Al Gore and Oliver North that weren't true? Snopes.com helped me learn the reality. This site is all about confirming or debunking the stories that race around the Internet every day. Look around Snopes, and be amazed.

UrbanLegends.about.com, a site run by the *New York Times*, is also helpful for sorting out paranoid nuttiness from truth.

FactCheck.org, a political fact-checking site, and its FactChecked.org companion site for students and teachers, will help you sort through a few of the political claims tossed around our republic. Your best bet, I'd suggest, is to assume that everything you see in any political advertisement is at best misleading, especially if it's an attack on a candidate or campaign.

QuackWatch.org is invaluable for debunkery of, you guessed it, bad information about health.

In the experimental category I'm a fan of MediaBugs.org (another project on which I serve as an advisor). Scott Rosenberg, with the help of people like you, is compiling a database of journalistic errors, including notes on whether or when the mistakes are corrected. If he can get enough buy-in from journalists at all levels in his early experiment in the San Francisco Bay Area, this could become a national resource of note.

Detecting Slant

The Center for Media and Democracy, which leans left politically, has created an invaluable information trove about the organizations that seek to persuade us to buy or believe. It's called SourceWatch, and I frequently check it out.

The mass media consistently misrepresent science and medicine. Ben Goldacre, a British doctor, writer and broadcaster, runs BadScience.net, where he routinely demolishes bad reporting in ways that help readers understand how they can be more discerning themselves. If you follow his work you'll more easily spot bad science reporting yourself.*

Fabrice Florin's project Newstrust.net, aimed at persuading communities of readers to grade reports based on a variety of criteria, is a promising approach. I encourage you to join and add your own knowledge to the database. (Note: I'm an advisor to the project.)

Again, this is the briefest of lists. The key point is that the more something matters to you—the more you have at stake—the more you need to investigate further. I'll be adding a fresher and more extensive list to mediactive.com.

---

*"I don't want to be a guy who says 'This is good and this is bad,'" Goldacre told me. Rather, he wants to help people understand how they can go about being more careful in their media consumption.

"The reality," he said, "is you'll never be able to have a set of rules for whether someone is reliable or not. What you can derive clearly are heuristics: time-saving devices and shortcuts. They are reasonably accurate, but they misfire sometimes. People try to game our heuristics. This is what quacks do when they buy fake doctorates.

"What's interesting about reading online with linked text is that heuristics become quicker. One of most powerful heuristics I use is whether someone writing about scientific research links to the original paper or at least to the press release. If not, I won't waste any time reading it."

Risks, Statistics, Lies

Asking yourself whether something makes sense is especially relevant in understanding risk. Journalists have been, as a trade, beyond negligent in explaining relative risks. Local television news, for example, has been almost criminal in its incessant hyping of crime even during times when crime rates were plummeting, helping persuade people that danger was growing when it was in fact shrinking. While the individual crimes and victims are all too real, the overall incidence of crime has been grossly overstated. And legislators, all too happy to "do something" in response to media-fed public fears, often pass laws, such as Draconian sentencing for non-violent crimes, that do much more aggregate harm than good.

Medical news reports, moreover, tend to vary from ill-informed to downright crazy; the unwillingness of a significant portion of the American population to get vaccinated for the H1N1 flu, based on paranoid rumors and media reports, is downright scary. Panic is often the greatest danger, because it leads to bad responses, and when the media fuel panic they are doing the greatest of disservices.

Statistics are a related problem. Too few people understand statistical methods or meaning. If you hear that such and such product or substance is linked to a 50 percent rise in some low-incidence disease, you need to also understand that the likelihood that you'll get that ailment remains vanishingly small.

These are issues of slant, not accuracy. But they have everything to do with our understanding of the world around us.

I can hear you asking this important question: Who has the time to look into all of this, anyway? No one does. But when you're looking at something you care about, or when you're just suspicious, isn't it worth taking a little extra time to check just a bit further?

The bottom line is to start with common sense. Heeding that first bit of skepticism can save you a lot of pain later.

Sidebar: The Wikipedia Question

In May 2009, the *Irish Times* reported a story that made journalists everywhere cringe. The article, entitled "Student's Wikipedia hoax quote used worldwide in newspaper obituaries," began:

> A Wikipedia hoax by a 22-year-old Dublin student resulted in a fake quote being published in newspaper obituaries around the world. The quote was attributed to French composer

Maurice Jarre who died at the end of March. It was posted on the online encyclopedia shortly after his death and later appeared in obituaries published in *The Guardian*, the London Independent, on the *BBC Music Magazine* website and in Indian and Australian newspapers.

Hoaxes are not new in journalism, but Wikipedia haters, who are vocal if not all that numerous, were thrilled with this one. It gave them another reason to attack the online encyclopedia.

Certainly, the site's relatively open nature was instrumental in the student's ability to pull off the hoax in the first place. But a closer examination, including a long note to readers by *The Guardian*—one of the publications that fell for the hoax—suggested a different lesson. In fact, as <u>Siobhain Butterworth</u>, the newspaper's "readers' editor," <u>observed</u>, the Wikipedia community performed well in a) discovering the lie and 2) fixing the article:

> Wikipedia editors were more skeptical about the unsourced quote [than newspaper editors who printed obituaries based on the false information]. They deleted it twice on 30 March and when Fitzgerald added it the second time it lasted only six minutes on the page. His third attempt was more successful— the quote stayed on the site for around 25 hours before it was spotted and removed again.

Still, the invented quote was widely used, and by people who should have known better. In *The Guardian*, there was apparently no citation, even to Wikipedia, which would have been a tip-off in the first instance.

As *The Guardian*'s Buttersworth also noted, "The moral of this story is not that journalists should avoid Wikipedia, but that they shouldn't use information they find there if it can't be traced back to a reliable primary source."

That applies to everyone, not just journalists. Wikipedia's <u>own policies</u> call for all information to be traced back to authoritative references, and articles are routinely flagged when they lack such references:

> Content should be verifiable with citations to reliable sources. Our editors' personal experiences, interpretations, or opinions do not belong here.

I say this again and again, to students and anyone else who'll listen:

*Wikipedia is often the best place to start, but the worst place to stop.**

It's the best place to start because you'll often find a solid article about a topic or person. It's the worst place to stop because that article might be wrong in some particular. A 2005 <u>article</u> in *Nature* magazine, comparing Wikipedia to the *Encyclopedia Britannica*, only muddied the issue, and not because it didn't conclusively resolve the question of which is more accurate. The point here is that you should not assume the particular fact you check at a particular moment is true.

But every decent Wikipedia article has something at the bottom that should also appear on newspaper articles online: a long list of links to original or at least credible outside sources, including news articles. And every Wikipedia article has a record of every change, down to the smallest detail, going back to the day it was first created.

Moreover, Wikipedia articles of any depth are accompanied by "meta" conversations about the articles themselves, where the editors discuss or argue among themselves about the quality of the information going into the articles and often about the credentials of the editors who have been making the latest changes.

Yes, use Wikipedia—and lots of other sources. Just make sure you understand both its advantages and its limitations. And if you see something that's wrong, fix it! (More on that ahead.)

Anonymous Versus Pseudonymous

As the 2008 presidential campaign wound down, a Fox News TV report relayed a variety of negative attacks on Sarah Palin, the Republican vice presidential candidate, that it attributed to members of presidential candidate John McCain's campaign staff. Palin denounced the attackers—all of whom had been granted anonymity—as cowards.

Palin was right to be angry. The TV report was a perfect example of why anonymous critics should not be taken seriously—in fact, of why they should usually be flatly disbelieved.

Anonymous sources are one of professional journalism's worst habits. Their constant appearance, especially in newspapers and broadcast news outlets that ought to know better, turns otherwise

---

*Who agrees with me? Jimmy Wales, Wikipedia's co-founder, among others. I'm posting a video interview with him on the Mediactive site where he says so. Note: He's a friend, and I'm an investor in his privately held company, Wikia.

respectable institutions into gossip mongers and invites audiences to doubt what they're being told.

Ombudsmen at the *Washington Post* and *New York Times* have repeatedly scolded their colleagues not just for their incessant use of anonymous sources, but also for the journalists' flouting of internal policies banning what they're doing. It makes no difference, apparently, because the "anonymice," as media critic Jack Shafer calls them, just keep on appearing.

Shafer notes that he's no absolutist on these things, understanding that in some kinds of situations anonymous sources are vital. We learned about the Bush administration's illegal wiretapping program against Americans because someone spilled it to the *New York Times* (though the newspaper unaccountably held the story for a year before publishing it). But before the U.S. invaded Iraq we also "learned" via anonymice quoted in the same paper—the quotation marks are deliberate—that Saddam Hussein's regime had weapons of mass destruction. These, of course, were lies laundered through the newspaper by an administration that was hell-bent to create a case for war.

One of the more ridiculous ways news organizations pretend to be more transparent about an inherently opaque practice is to offer reasons why the sources can't allow themselves to be identified by name.

Occasionally it makes sense, as a former Times Reader representative, Clark Hoyt, noted when a Good Samaritan at a New York assault didn't want his name published because the assailant was still at large. But Hoyt was too much the gentleman when he termed "baffling" a story in which a source was granted anonymity "because he was discussing drug-testing information."

I have a rule of thumb. When a news report quotes anonymous sources, I immediately question the entire thing. I'm skeptical enough about spin from people who stand behind their own words, but downright cynical about the people who use journalist-granted anonymity to push a position or, worse, slam someone else.

When someone hides behind anonymity to attack someone else, you shouldn't just ignore it. *In the absence of actual evidence, you should actively disbelieve it.* And you should hold the journalist who reports it in contempt for being the conduit.

New media are a wider world of anonymous and semi-anonymous claims and attacks. The blogger who refuses to identify himself or herself invites me to look elsewhere, unless I'm persuaded by a great deal of evidence that there's good reason to stick around. And, as I said earlier, the anonymous commenters on blogs or news articles deserve less than no credibility on any BS meter; they deserve to start in deep minus territory. Where would I put the attacks on Palin? Well, given the sources (Fox and the anonymous people launching these verbal grenades), I'd start below zero and wait for some evidence.

Pseudonyms are a more interesting case, and can have value. Done right, they can bring greater accountability and therefore somewhat more credibility than anonymous comments. Content-management systems have mechanisms designed to require some light-touch registration, even if it's merely having a working email address, and to prevent more than one person from using the same pseudonym on a given site. A pseudonym isn't as useful as a real name, but it does encourage somewhat better behavior, in part because it's more accountable. A pseudonymous commenter who builds a track record of worthwhile conversation, moreover, can build personal credibility even without revealing his or her real name (though I believe using real names is almost always better.)

Ultimately, as we'll discuss later, conveners of online conversations need to provide better tools for the people having the conversations. These include moderation systems that actually help bring the best commentary to the surface, ways for readers to avoid the postings of people they find offensive, and community-driven methods of identifying and banning abusers.

For all this, I want to emphasize again that we should preserve anonymity when used responsibly, and appreciate why it's vital. Anonymity protects whistle-blowers and others for whom speech can be unfairly dangerous.

But when people don't stand behind their words, a reader should always wonder why and make appropriate adjustments.

Talking with Journalists (of All Kinds)

More and more print journalists are posting their email addresses in the work they publish. They are acknowledging their role in a broadening, emergent media ecosystem, recognizing that news is becoming a conversation instead of a lecture. (Broadcast reporters, for the most part, aren't nearly so willing to join conversations; their loss.)

Mainstream journalists are congenitally thin-skinned; insecurity seems almost a precondition to employment in traditional newsrooms. This has always been a notable irony, given that the journalism business routinely shoots people off their pedestals, often after helping install them there in the first place. So when you contact a journalist, you're likely to get him or her to listen if you're polite; attack mode is almost always the wrong approach.

The best journalists do want to listen, and sometimes they even want your help. In Ft. Myers, Florida, the local newspaper asked its readers for help on a local story involving the water and sewer system. The readers responded, and the newspaper was able to do much better journalism as a result.

Joshua Micah Marshall, creator of the Talking Points Memo collection of political and policy blogs, has done much of the best work in this arena. He regularly asks his readers for help poring through documents or asking questions of public officials. (In a later chapter I'll describe how journalists could do this as a matter of routine, and the kinds of results we might get.)

The ProPublica.org investigative site, meanwhile, has asked its users to add their expertise in a variety of ways. Its 2009 "Stimulus Spot Check"—a deeper look at whether and how states were using road and bridge construction money from the federal economic stimulus package enacted earlier in the year—was assisted by dozens of volunteers from the site's ProPublica Reporting Network. The professional journalists obtained a random sample of the approved projects and asked the volunteers to help assess what had happened.

If you live in a community with particularly smart media organizations, you may be able to join them in a more formal way. American Public Media's Public Insight Network, best known for its work in Minnesota and the upper Midwest, has signed up some 70,000 people who've agreed to be sounding boards and sources for the journalism created by professionals (and ultimately, one hopes, the citizens themselves).

The New Media Watchdogs

In the previous chapter we noted the sad state of media criticism in traditional circles and the heartening rise of online media criticism. We should do more to make it an integral part of mediactivism.

If you're not a fan of *The Daily Show*'s media criticism, you're just not paying attention. Jon Stewart and his producers routinely skewer the media, often beating traditional media and bloggers alike to the punch; the program scooped everyone with the news in November 2009 that Sean Hannity's Fox News program had, as *Daily Show* producer Ramin Hedayati told PoynterOnline, "used footage from Glenn Beck's 9/12 rally to make his [November health-care] rally look bigger.... We were surprised that no one else caught it." (Just an inadvertent mistake, Hannity later said after admitting it.) It's a commentary in itself that, according to several surveys, many younger adults say they get a great deal of their news from *The Daily Show*.

Some of the best and most ardent online criticism is coming from political partisans, though you have to keep in mind that they're criticizing from a distinctly one-sided platform and adjust your expectations accordingly. Sites such as Media Matters for America are earning big audiences with their dedication, as that site proclaims, "to comprehensively monitoring, analyzing, and correcting conservative misinformation in the U.S. media." The site's stated bias helps us understand its reports, which strike me as some of the most thorough of their kind, especially in their deconstructions of television news and commentary. While Media Matters is prone to hyperbole in interpreting the facts, as far as I can tell it rigorously checks those facts. Likewise, George Mason University's Stats site, with a firmly libertarian-right world view, does useful analysis of media misuse of statistics.

People and organizations with grievances about the way they've been covered have better options than ever before. It's increasingly common for companies and public figures to tell their side of stories on their own sites. Intriguingly, the Obama White House embarked on a media-criticism campaign of its own early on, specifically taking on Fox News as a propaganda machine, not a "real" journalism organization. Whether a president should be arguing with individual news operations is a separate issue, but I welcomed the administration's effort to explain to Americans what people paying attention had already learned.

Bigger media organizations have legions of critics. (You can even find a long Wikipedia article devoted solely to criticism of the *New York Times*.) Yet even in smaller cities and towns, you're likely to find someone (ideally, several people) blogging about local media. Remember the credibility scale, of course, when you read the critiques. But do read them, and decide as the facts shake out which ones are worth continuing to read.

Some might argue we have too much media criticism in a world where bloggers are constantly on the attack against what they perceive, often accurately, as inadequate journalism. But one of the healthier aspects of the rise of bloggers as media watchdogs has been the way journalists have had to start developing thicker skins—not ignoring their critics, but also not reacting with the pure defensiveness of the past. Professionals still tend to be sensitive about all this.

Happily, at least a few have started listening, and are joining the conversation on their own blogs, Twitter streams and elsewhere. The truth is that we need even more media criticism, at every level.

What drives traditional journalists especially crazy is being attacked unfairly. (Pot, meet kettle….) Comment threads under big media articles, which are so often unmoderated wastelands of evil spewings from near-sociopaths, become Exhibit A for journalists who don't want to participate in conversations with readers. So the bias, even today, is to stay away from genuine contact with audiences. While media people are joining some conversations, they're still avoiding genuine discussion of their own failings.

Bloggers often have skins as thin as any traditional journalist's, and some have a tendency to respond to even mild critiques with the kind of fury that only makes them look worse. But bloggers also have an instant feedback mechanism that traditional media people rarely use: the comments. You almost never find a mass-media journalist participating in the comments on his or her organization's website. Bloggers do tend to participate on their own sites, and on Twitter and other forums.

Escape the Echo Chamber

One of the great worries about the Internet is the echo chamber effect: the notion that democratized media have given us a way to pay attention only to the people we know we'll agree with, paying no attention to contrary views or, often, reality.

This is no idle worry. But the same digital media that make it possible to retreat into our own beliefs give us easier ways to emerge, and engage.

A key principle introduced in the first chapter was the idea of going outside your comfort zone. This has several, related facets:

- Learn from people who live in places and cultures entirely different from your own.

- Listen to the arguments of people you know you'll disagree with.

- Challenge your own assumptions.

You need to be somewhat systematic about the first and second of those points, but also opportunistic. While I make it a point to read political blogs written by people who make my blood boil, and read journalism from other parts of the world, I also make the best possible use of that elemental unit of the Web: the hyperlink.

Even the most partisan bloggers typically point to the work they are pounding into the sand. If a left-wing blogger writes, "So and so, the blithering idiot, is claiming such and such," he links to the such and such he's challenging—and you can click that link to see what so and so actually said. Contrast this with what happens when you watch, say, Fox News or MSNBC on televison. The TV set, at least today's version, doesn't come with links; and clearly the commentators don't want you to consider world views other than their own.

The link culture of the Web is part of the antidote to the echo chamber. But you have to click. Do it, often.

If you do, there's a good chance you'll discover, from time to time, that you either didn't have a sufficiently deep understanding of something, or what you thought was simply wrong. There's nothing bad about changing your mind; only shallow people never do so.

I engage in a semi-annual exercise that started more than a decade ago, when I was writing for the *San Jose Mercury News*, Silicon Valley's daily newspaper. I kept a list in the back of a desk drawer, entitled "Things I Believe"—a 10-point list of topics about which I'd come to previous conclusions. They weren't moral or ethical in nature. Rather, they were issue-oriented, and about my job as a business and technology columnist. Every six months or so, I'd go down the list and systematically attack every proposition, looking for flaws in what I'd previously taken for granted.

For example, one longstanding item on my list was this: "Microsoft is an abusive monopoly that threatens innovation, and government antitrust scrutiny is essential." From 1994 until I left the *Mercury News* in 2005, I continued to believe this was true, though a shade less so by the end of that period than at the beginning and during the software company's most brutal, predatory era. Since then, though, conditions have changed. Given the rise of Google and other Web-based enterprises, not to mention Apple's growing power and the controlling and anticompetitive behavior of the huge telecommunications companies, I've modified my views about what the chief tech-world worries should be. Microsoft is still powerful and sometimes abusive, but it's not nearly the threat it once was. (No, I don't make my list public, though I talk about many of its points in my Mediactive blog from time to time, which is almost the same thing.) The next time I update the list, I'll probably move Apple above Microsoft on my list of companies worth watching closely in this way.

Consider creating your own list of "givens" that you will challenge on a regular basis. This is especially vital when it comes to political beliefs. My basic political grounding combines elements of liberal, conservative and libertarian doctrine, and I vote according to a collection of issues, not remotely by party. But I'm constantly reassessing.

The late Carl Sagan, in a wonderful essay called "The Fine Art of Baloney Detection," put it this way:

> Try not to get overly attached to a hypothesis just because it's yours. It's only a way station in the pursuit of knowledge. Ask yourself why you like the idea. Compare it fairly with the alternatives. See if you can find reasons for rejecting it. If you don't, others will.

Chapter 4

Journalism's Evolving Ecosystem

Think of this chapter a relatively brief but important digression. One goal is to persuade you that we still need journalism, no matter who's going to do it. I also want to suggest, in the process, that we're going to have to expand our understanding of the media and journalistic ecosystems, because many more of us are participating—and all of us can participate—in this new world of media and information.

Let me reassure you, as I did in the introduction, that I'm not trying to turn you into a journalist. But I will, in later chapters, urge you to be a contributing member of the media ecosystem, not just a consumer, and in ways that provide useful, trustworthy information to others.

For now, though, let's use the words "journalism" and "journalist" to explore the part of the overall media ecosystem that we all want to be useful and trustworthy. Let's start by asking a question I hear all the time:

Who is a journalist?

You've already guessed, I hope, that this is the Wrong Question.

Here's the right one:

What is journalism?

This is more than semantics. Asking the question in the right way has real-world implications. The language of so-called "press shield laws," for example, aims to protect whistle-blowers and the journalists whom they tell about government or corporate wrongdoing. But as we'll discuss in the next chapter, these laws could offer false comfort by narrowly defining what a "journalist" is and leaving out a huge range of people and institutions that effectively practice journalism nowadays. The goal should be to protect the act of journalism, as opposed to the people declared to be journalists.

I hope we can agree that the *New York Times* is journalism. Ditto BBC News. Sometimes they get things wrong—even badly wrong—but they do journalism.

I also hope we can agree that the "Blah Blah Blah" blog (actually, there are quite a few blogs with that name!) and the YouTube video of "Nat and Foxy disco dancing" are not journalism. They may be interesting to their small audiences, and we should celebrate the fact that someone is trying to be creative. But they're not journalism.

If we dig deeper into new media, the answer starts to get complicated. Some of what appeared on my former neighborhood email list was journalism; most wasn't. But consider the Talking Points Memo collection of blogs, founded by Joshua Micah Marshall. They're online only, and they have a politically left-of-center world view, but they are so unquestionably journalism that they've won a George Polk Award, one of the craft's truly prestigious honors.

Consider also Brad DeLong, a former Clinton administration Treasury Department official who teaches at the University of California at Berkeley, writes a brilliant blog about policy and many other things. He does something that surely looks like journalism: commentary informed by knowledge.

Or take what happened during a Christmas Day blizzard in 2009: people posted local road conditions and information about where stranded travelers could hunker down with local families. Even if that can't be called journalism in a traditional sense, it's certainly more useful to a family in a sedan on the side of the road, using a phone that has a Web browser, than any roundup story by a news organization.

Thanks to the Digital Age tools available to all of us, many institutions never known for journalism are now contributing information with powerful journalistic impact. These almost-journalists include the Council on Foreign Relations and some advocacy organizations that do deep research and present it with care, including the ACLU and Human Rights Watch.

Any one of us can, and many of us will, commit an act of journalism. We may contribute to the journalism ecosystem once, rarely, frequently or constantly. How we deal with these contributions—deciding to make one; what we do with what we've created; and how we use what others have created—is complex and evolving. But this is the future.

Citizen Journalism Defines Its Future

When I wrote *We the Media* in 2004, I was confident that citizen journalism would become an essential part of the ecosystem. Nothing I've seen leads me to believe otherwise. But the genre has a long way to go.

What is citizen journalism, specifically? There's no single definition, just as we can't restrict traditional journalism to what people do in newspapers. There are a thousand examples (and we point to them all the time on the Mediactive blog), but the important thing to recognize is the sheer variety, in format, style and intent. Remember, we are talking about what is journalism, not who's a journalist.

As I'll discuss in this chapter, citizen journalism and citizen media in general have drawn increasing attention from investors and media partners. Foundations, too, have stepped up to fill at least some of the perceived and real gaps in news, and have put millions of dollars into initiatives of, by and for the people.

It has also been heartening to watch traditional media organizations, big and small, begin to understand why they need to play a role in this arena. The vast majority of newspapers now have staff blogs, which is a good start, and as noted in Chapter 3 a few forward-looking organizations are inviting their audiences to participate in the actual journalism. But Old Media continues to be behind the curve, and I don't see that changing much.

What is unquestionably changing, at an accelerating pace, is the take-up by people everywhere of the professionals' tools of trade. In one area, photojournalism, a transition of unprecedented magnitude is well under way.

"Spot News" Becomes Citizen Journalism

People have been witnessing and taking pictures of notable events for a long, long time. And they've been selling them to traditional news organizations for just as long.

But professional photojournalists, and more recently videographers, have continued to make good livings at a craft that helps inform the rest of us about the world we live in. That craft has never been more vibrant, or more vital. But the ability to make a living at it is crumbling.

The pros who deal in breaking news have a problem: They can't possibly compete in the mediasphere of the future. We're entering a world of ubiquitous media creation and access. When the tools of creation and access are so profoundly democratized, many (if not most) of the pros will find themselves fighting a losing battle to save their careers.

Let's do a little time travel. An old-fashioned movie camera captured the most famous pictures in the citizen-media genre: the assassination of President John F. Kennedy in Dallas, Texas on November 22, 1963. Abraham Zapruder, the man pointing the camera that day in Dealey Plaza, sold the film to *Life Magazine* for $150,000— over a million dollars in today's currency.

In Dealey Plaza that day, one man happened to capture a motion picture—somewhat blurred but utterly gruesome nonetheless—of those terrible events. Zapruder's work, by any standard we can imagine, was an act of citizen journalism, even though the term did not exist back then.

Now note what media tools people carry around with them routinely today—or, better yet, what they'll have a decade from now. And then transport yourself, and those tools, back to 1963.

Dozens or hundreds of people in Dealey Plaza would have been capturing high-definition videos of the assassination, most likely via their camera-equipped mobile phones as well as single-purpose digital cameras and video recorders. They'd have been capturing those images from multiple perspectives. And—this is key—all of those devices would have been attached to digital networks.

If the soon-to-be-ubiquitous technology had been in use back in 1963, several things are clear. One is that videos of this event would have been posted online almost instantly. Professional news organizations, which would also have had their own videos, would have been competing with a blizzard of other material almost from the start—and given traditional media's usually appropriate reluctance to broadcast the most gruesome images (e.g., the beheading of the American businessman Nick Berg in Iraq), the online accounts might well have been a primary source.

And think about this: We'd also soon have a three-dimensional hologram of the event, given the number of cameras capturing it from various angles. Which means we'd probably know for sure whether someone was shooting at the president from that famous grassy knoll. In the future, government commissions will still issue official reports, but the documents will be created with much more input from citizens, who, because of digital media tools, are playing increasingly direct roles in governance as well as elections. The prospect of actually making policy, or at least having an impact on it, can offer a serious incentive to be a citizen journalist.

Another famous picture of our times is the single image that we will most remember from the July 2005 bombings in London. It was taken by Adam Stacey inside the Underground (London's subway), as he and others escaped from a smoky train immediately after one of the bombs exploded.

The production values of the image were hardly professional, but that didn't matter. What did matter was the utter authenticity of the image, made so by the fact that the man was there at the right time with the right media-creation gear.

In a world of ubiquitous media tools, which is almost here, someone will be on the spot at every significant event. It might well be you, and you should be prepared for the moment when you are in that position, which I'll discuss in the next section.

How can people who cover breaking news for a living begin to compete? They can't possibly be everywhere at once. They can compete only on the stories where they are physically present—and, in the immediate future, by being relatively trusted sources. But the fact remains that there are far more newsworthy situations than pro photographers. In the past, most of those situations were never captured. This is no longer the case.

Is it so sad that the professionals will have more trouble making a living this way in coming years? To them, it must be—and I have friends in the business, which makes this painful to write in some ways. To the rest of us, as long as we get the trustworthy news we need, the trend is more positive.

Remember, there was once a fairly healthy community of portrait painters. When photography came along, a lot of them had to find other work, or at least their ranks were not refilled when they retired. Professional portrait photographers, similarly, are less in demand today than they were a generation ago. But portraits have survived—and thrived.

The photojournalist's job may be history before long. But photojournalism has never been more important, or more widespread. You can be a part of it, and I hope you will.

Advocates: The Almost-Journalists

Newspapers, magazines and broadcast news aren't the only places where deep investigative journalism is to be found. Nonpartisan think tanks and not-for-profit organizations do a lot of it. For example, the "Crisis Guides" published by the Council on Foreign Relations provide remarkably detailed coverage of global political crises—the council's report on the genocide in Darfur is a great example. As the judges of the Knight-Batten Awards said of the council when honoring its work, "This is an institution stepping up and honoring the best of journalism. It's filling an absolutely articulated need."

Others are also helping to fill this need, even if what they're doing isn't, strictly speaking, journalism. Call them the advocates.

Journalism at its most basic level is a combination of two essential tasks. The first is reporting: gathering information via research, interviews, etc. The second part is telling people what you've learned: writing (in the broadest sense, including video, audio, graphics and more) and editing.

So, by these notions, what famous journalism organization has done some of the best reporting about the United States Government's Guantanamo Bay prison? That's the place where the United States holds the people the government has declared to be terrorists, a prison where prisoners have been in many cases tortured and, until recently, held without access to the legal system.

With a few exceptions, notably at the McClatchy Newspapers Washington Bureau and the *New York Times*, the people who've done the best reporting on this scandal have not, for the most part, been working for major media outfits. They've been working for that famous journalism organization called the American Civil Liberties Union.

Yes, the ACLU—a passionate advocate for the Bill of Rights—has done prodigious work to uncover the truth about America's actions in creating this extra-legal system. And on the ACLU's "Rights in Detention" sub-site, you'll find a huge amount of information—and advocacy—about this topic.

As my Salon.com colleague Glenn Greenwaldobserved in 2008:

> It has been left to the ACLU and similar groups (such as the Center for Constitutional Rights and Electronic Frontier Foundation) to uncover what our Government is doing precisely because the institutions whose responsibility that is—the "opposition party," the Congress, the Intelligence Committees, the press—have failed miserably in those duties.

Now consider Human Rights Watch, whose mission is "Defending Human Rights Worldwide." This is another advocacy organization that does superb reporting on the issues it cares about. Its report on Saudi Arabian domestic workers, for example, is an exhaustively researched document on some troubling practices. This is incredibly fine reporting.

Smaller advocacy organizations are becoming more active in this sphere, too. The Goldwater Institute, an Arizona think tank named after conservative patron saint Barry Goldwater, hired an investigative journalist in 2009. Since then, Mark Flatten has produced several noteworthy "watchdog" reports on local government matters.

Recall the public-knowledge trajectory an organization like the ACLU had to follow in the past. It would do painstaking research on topics like Guantanamo, and then issue reports. When a new report was released, the organization's researchers or public relations people would contact reporters at, say, the *New York Times* and hope that the newspaper would write a story about it. If the national press ignored the report, no matter how powerful the content, the information would reach only a tiny number of people.

The ACLU still works hard to get its reports covered by the *Times* and other national media organizations. The traditional media retain a powerful role in helping the public learn about important issues. But advocates have new avenues, which they are learning to use more effectively. They'd be even more effective, I believe, if they applied the principles of journalism to their work—principles I'll be discussing in detail in the next several chapters.

The productions by the ACLU, Human Rights Watch and many similar advocacy organizations are what I'm calling "almost-journalism." Their reporting is superb, but what they produce tends to fall just a shade short of journalism—not always, but often enough that this caveat is necessary.

Are they part of the media? Yes. They are absolutely in the media field now, because they are using the tools of media creation to learn and tell stories, and to make those stories available to a wide audience. These organizations and countless others like them—small and large, local and international—are part of the media ecosystem. With just a little extra effort, they could be part of the journalistic ecosystem too, in ways that go far beyond their traditional roles.

The area where they fall the shortest is the one that comes hardest to advocates: fairness. This is a broad and somewhat fuzzy word, and we'll spend some time on it in an upcoming chapter. But it means, in general, that you a) listen hard to people who disagree with you, b) hunt for facts and data that are contrary to your own stand, and c) reflect disagreements and nuances in what you tell the rest of us.

Advocacy journalism has a long and honorable history. The best in this arena have always acknowledged the disagreements and nuances, and they've been fair in reflecting opposing or diverging views and ideas.

By doing so, they can strengthen their own arguments. At the very least, they are clearer, if not absolutely clear, on the other sides' arguments. (That's sides, not side; almost everything has more than two sides.)

Of course, transparency is essential in this process, and for the most part we get that from advocacy groups. The ones we can't trust are the ones that take positions that echo the views of their financial patrons. The think-tank business is known for this kind of thing, as we've seen earlier, and it's an abysmal practice.

As the traditional journalism business continues to implode, the almost-journalists will come to play an increasingly important role in the media ecosystem. With traditional journalism companies firing reporters and editors right and left, the almost-journalist organizations have both the deep pockets and the staffing to fill in some of the gap—if they can find a way to apply fairness and transparency to their media, whether it's designed to inform or to advocate.

Like everything else, this notion gets serious pushback. Ethan Zuckerman notes that Human Rights Watch competes for foundation funding with actual journalism organizations such as his own Global Voices Online project. He also says that helping the almost-journalists doesn't solve the question of who will pay for journalism, but rather shifts it one level away from the reader/viewer/listener.

I can't dispute what he says, but I still think NGO-almost-journalism is worthy of the public's careful attention.

Ultimately, this conversation is about who deserves to be listened to. New York University professor Jay Rosen defines it elegantly. In a talk he gave to budding French journalists, he said:

> Your authority starts with, "I'm there, you're not, let me tell you about it." If "anyone" can produce media and share it with the world, what makes the pro journalist special, or worth listening to? Not the press card, not the by-line, not the fact of employment by a major media company. None of that. The most reliable source of authority for a professional journalist will continue to be what James W. Carey called "the idea of a report." That's when you can truthfully say to the users, "I'm there, you're not, let me tell you about it." Or, "I was at the demonstration, you weren't, let me tell you how the cops behaved." Or, altering my formula slightly, "I interviewed the workers who were on that oil drilling platform when it exploded, you didn't, let me tell you what they said." Or, "I reviewed those documents, you didn't, let me tell you what I found." Your authority begins when you do the work. If an amateur or a blogger does the work, the same authority is earned.

Your Contribution to the Journalism Ecosystem

Many of the people who were near the famous Minnesota bridge collapse in August 2007 followed an instinct to run toward the bridge, not away from it, so they could capture videos and still images of the wreckage. Within hours, hundreds of <u>photos</u> had been posted to the Flickr photo sharing site, and dozens of <u>videos</u> were on YouTube.

As I write this in late December 2009, I'm watching the latest citizen-journalism <u>videos</u> made with mobile phones at anti-government protests in Iran. It has taken genuine bravery for these people to stay on scene during the mayhem and tell the world what they're seeing.

I don't want to suggest that everyone reading this book is going to commit regular acts of journalism. Most of us won't, and that's fine.

But as I noted earlier, I do hope you'll be thinking about being ready if that moment arrives.

What should you do when you witness something that may be newsworthy? Let's assume, for the moment, that you're carrying a mobile phone with a camera in it.

First, get the picture or video, if you can do so safely. If it's risky, understand the risks and make a decision accordingly.

Second, know what you can do next. The modern instinct, if you don't have your own blog or other site of your own, is to post it on a photo or video site, or to send it to CNN. Maybe we should rethink several current assumptions in this process.

People have been putting themselves in harm's way to "get the picture" for as long as cameras have been around. Some—the professional photojournalists—have been paid for it, but others have not.

I question the ethics of news organizations that invite submissions from the public without doing their utmost to warn non-paid shooters away from risks. It's one thing for a news channel staffer to get videos inside the hurricane, but quite another to urge the same from a resident who'd be safer remaining indoors.

I also question the ethics of news organizations that assume, as many do, that the work of the citizen journalist is something the company should get for free. I'm highly skeptical of business models, typically conceived by Big Media companies, that tell the rest of us: "You do all the work, and we'll take all the money we make by exploiting it." This is not just unethical, it's also unsustainable in the long run, because the people who give freely of their time won't be satisfied to see mega-corporations rake in the financial value of what others have created.

Not every person who captures a newsworthy image or video necessarily wants to be paid. But many do, and right now, for the most part, their compensation is a pat on the back. Eventually, someone will come up with a robust business model that puts a welcome dent into this modern version of sharecropping.

Stacey's picture in the London Underground was widely distributed—it was published on the front pages of many newspapers—in part because he put it out under a <u>Creative Commons</u> license allowing anyone the right to use it in any way provided that they attributed the picture to its creator. There were misunderstandings (including at least one use by a photo agency that apparently claimed at least partial credit for itself), but the copyright terms—I'll explain Creative Commons more fully in the Epilogue—almost certainly helped spread it far and wide in a very short time.

Beyond licensing, we need new market systems to reward citizen photographers. Some startups are positioning themselves as brokers, including a service called <u>Demotix</u>. As I'll also discuss later, we need to take the next step to a real-time auction system.

A few news organizations have adapted, and are finding ways to reward citizen creators in tangible ways. <u>Bild</u>, the German tabloid, asks people to send in their own pictures, and pays for the ones it publishes. This is an important part of our future.

You Can Participate in Other Ways

Again, I don't expect you to suddenly decide to become a journalist. I do hope you've gained, in the past few chapters, a deeper appreciation for the craft and the people who practice it honorably. Maybe you'll be one of them from time to time.

Even if you never commit a single act of journalism, though, it's important to understand that being literate in today's world means more than just smarter consumption, however actively you do that.

Being literate is also about creating, contributing and collaborating. In the Digital Age, participation is part of genuine literacy. As Jay Rosen said, your authority begins when you do the work. Remember that as you read the next few chapters, where we'll look at what this means, and how you can participate—at whatever level feels best to you.

Part II: Introduction

Chances are you're already creating media. If you have a Facebook account, you're a media creator—at least in the sense I'm talking about here. If you send emails to more than one person at a time to let them know about interesting things, or participate in any kind of online forum, you're a media creator. If you post photos or videos anywhere online, you're a media creator. If you do any number of things with the digital tools at your disposal, count yourself in the creative ranks.

Using media actively this way, in contrast to consuming it passively, as was the norm in the last half of the 20th century, means more than being a better consumer. The Digital Age brings us new opportunities to be fully literate—and the creative act is an essential part. The chapters in Part II will help you make the most of being an active user of the media that the Digital Age has thrust upon all of us.

As I've said earlier in this book, I'm not expecting you to become a journalist. But I'll strongly suggest, even at the risk of being a little pushy, that you learn the principles of journalism. This will bring you enormous benefit, especially in understanding our messy media landscape.

These principles are also useful, of course, if you are going to make your own media at any level. They're useful, that is, if you are trying to help other people understand their world (or yours) a little better—and if you want them to trust what you say. They've provided a bedrock for the best news and information from the folks who get paid to provide it, and they're just as helpful for you and me.

Whatever the level of your contribution to the new media landscape, even it it's just among friends, it's good to think about some issues beyond the obvious ones, such as whether to blog or just use Facebook. I want to help you understand why I believe you need your own presence on the Internet beyond just a Facebook page, and a few of the wrinkles to consider in establishing your own presence in cyberspace.

I'll also try to fit *your* creative activity into the overall landscape of tomorrow's information ecosystem, and offer some ideas on how it'll evolve. Hint: It's going to be messy, but also exciting.

The chapters in this part of the book present options for creating media that range from the simple to the quite sophisticated. If you're not very far along, and a chapter goes beyond what you want to know, just skip ahead to the next chapter. But mark your place—after you've been active for a while you might very well want to come back and read about the next steps. I certainly hope you will.

Chapter 5

Principles of Trustworthy Media Creation

The 2009 <u>videos</u> were dramatic, capturing several employees of ACORN, the housing-advocacy organization, apparently offering their help to clients on how to set up a brothel and evade any number of laws.

Using hidden cameras, conservative <u>activists</u> had gone undercover to capture conversations that led to a political uproar and Congressional action against the advocacy group. The creators of the videos made no secret of their goal: to "get" ACORN and expose it as a corrupt organization.

They called themselves journalists, and there was an element of journalism in their reports—though the videos were later <u>revealed</u> to have been edited in massively misleading ways. But when one of the creators of the ACORN videos was later <u>arrested</u> in New Orleans on charges that he'd attempted to spy on a Democratic senator, his journalistic bona fides disappeared entirely.

If you venture into anything resembling journalism, I hope you'll be more honorable than that crowd.

This chapter addresses people who are ready to go beyond purely personal or speculative blogs or occasional appearances on YouTube and the like. It's for those who have become mediactive consumers and now want to apply mediactive principles to their own creative work online, especially if their intent is to provide useful information to other people.

Important: What you'll be reading in the next few pages may seem like it's intended only for professional journalists. I'll be happy if some of them do read what follows, because lord knows that too many have forgotten or abandoned some vital principles.

But even though I do plan to talk quite a bit about what they do—and will be quite critical about how some have done their jobs in recent years—I hope you'll read what follows in the context of what you might be doing to create your own media now and in the future. These are universal principles, not just for people who call themselves journalists but for anyone who wants to be trusted for what they say or write. They are for all of us in a mediactive world, and the more you hope to be taken seriously, the more I hope you'll appreciate them.

Like the active-consumer principles in Chapter 2—the bedrock on which these creation principles rest—they add up to being honorable. In brief, they involve:

- Thoroughness
- Accuracy
- Fairness
- Independence
- Transparency

Transparency is the most difficult principle for traditional media organizations, even though it's relatively common among bloggers. In the end, however, it may be the most important of all, so I'm making it a major focus of this chapter. I find that I'm advocating it more and more ardently in all kinds of communication, from blogs to the BBC.*

Let's look at the principles in more detail. You'll see that they blur into each other at times, just as the principles for media consumers overlap. As I did with those, I'll flesh out some of the tactics to live up these principles in the next chapter.

1. Be Thorough

In Chapter 2, I stressed the importance of asking more questions. Whether you're asking so you can be better informed or so you can inform others, the digital world gives us nearly infinite tools for reporting, defined here as the gathering of information or just plain learning about various things. But none of these tools can replace old-fashioned methods such as making phone calls, conducting in-person interviews and visiting libraries. People can do shoddy research online or off, but the learning opportunities provided today by online communications and resources remove almost any excuse for lack of background knowledge.

---

*You'll notice that I don't list "objectivity" as a principle for creators of journalism. It's an ideal rather than a principle, and it's impossible to achieve—no human being is or can be truly objective. We can get closer to this ideal now than ever before, in part because the Internet's built-in capacity for collaboration makes it easier to find counterpoints to our own views and for our critics to find us (and then for us to respond). Author and Net researcher (and friend) David Weinberger calls transparency "the new objectivity," but I believe all of the principles in my list help us approach the ideal of objectivity.

You can't know everything, but good professional reporters serve as a good model: They try to learn as much as they can about whatever topic they're working on. It's better to know much more than you publish than to leave big holes in your story. The best reporters always want to make one more phone call, to check with one more source.

I had a rule of thumb as a reporter. I felt confident that I'd done enough reporting if my story used roughly 10 percent of what I knew. That is, I preferred to be so overloaded with facts and information that I had to be extremely selective, not to hide things but to write only what really mattered.

The Web offers all sorts of excellent material about how to do research. I'll list a bunch of these resources on the Mediactive website (mediactive.com), but take a look, for starters, at the University of Washington Libraries' "Research 101" site and the excellent News University collection at the Poynter Institute.

Online, we can take our research in amazing new directions, in particular by inviting others to be part of the discovery process. We can tell people what we're working on and ask them for help. "Crowdsourcing," which in journalism takes the form of asking the audience for help, has bolstered journalists' research on many levels, but it's only one of a number of ways to improve our reporting.

Let's spend a minute on the in-person interview. It's not easy to ask a stranger for information (at least, not for most people). It's even harder to ask probing questions. There are only two questions you should always ask, right at the end: 1) Is there anyone else I should talk to about this?, and 2) What didn't I ask that I should have asked, and what's the answer?

It's also important to remember that a lot of what we need to understand about the world can only be found in libraries, county courthouses and the like, and we should remember that those dusty paper stacks and files have plenty of value. Google can't digitize everything—not yet, anyway.

New facts and nuances often emerge after articles are published. One of Wikipedia's best characteristics is its recognition that we can liberate ourselves from the publication or broadcast metaphors made familiar during the age of literally manufactured media, where the paper product or tape for broadcasting was the end of the process. We may not get it totally right collectively—in fact, humans almost never get anything entirely right—but we can get closer as we assemble new data and nuances. I'll discuss this further in Chapter 7.

2. Be Accurate

Factual errors—especially those that are easily and clearly avoidable—do more to undermine trust than almost any other failing. Accuracy is the starting point for all solid information. While it's understandable that errors occur, given deadline pressures, it's disheartening that even in long-form journalism, such as magazines with human fact-checkers, some major and silly mistakes still make their way into articles. And it's stunning that professionals get things wrong when a simple Google check could have prevented the goof.

But accuracy rests on the bedrock of thoroughness, which takes time. It means, simply put: Check your facts, then check them again. Know where to look to verify claims or to separate fact from fiction. And never, ever, spell someone's name wrong.

In my first daily-newspaper job I spelled the name of a company wrong throughout an entire article, and didn't discover this until after publication. My mistake was simple: I got it wrong on first use as I wrote the story, and then, with the misspelling ingrained in my head, repeated the mistake every subsequent time. I didn't go back and check. The next morning, my editor called me into a small conference room, pointed out the error—the company's owner had called the paper—and told me, "You're better than this." I felt about one foot tall. I abjectly apologized to the owner of the company, who took it with amazingly good humor, and I learned a lesson.

That story is relevant to all of us. If you're applying for a job and your resume and/or cover letter are full of misspellings or outright inaccuracies, your application is likely to sink to the bottom of the pile. When people blog about me, one of the surest ways I know whether to pay attention is to see how they spelled my name. If they get it wrong, as so many do because they don't check, I'm not terribly inclined to take the rest of what they say all that seriously.

Getting it right means asking questions until you think you may know too much. Smart journalists know, moreover, that there are no stupid questions. Sometimes there are lazy questions, such as asking someone for information that you could easily have looked up; asking a lazy question will not endear you to the person you're interviewing. But if you don't understand something, you should just ask for an explanation. I enjoy being the person at a press conference who asks an obvious question that other reporters are too embarrassed to ask, for fear of seeming ill-informed. I'd rather have someone snicker at me for being a newbie than get something wrong.

When I was writing my newspaper technology column, I frequently called sources back after interviews to read them a sentence or paragraph of what I planned to write, so they could tell me whether I'd succeeded in explaining their technical work in plain English. Usually I had it right, but sometimes a source would correct me or offer a nuance. This made the journalism better, and made my sources trust me more.

Accuracy online extends past publication. You should invite your readers to let you know when they spot an error. MediaBugs' Scott Rosenberg and Regret the Error's Craig Silverman are working on a Web initiative to encourage publishers to put a prominent link on their pages, giving readers a way to report errors in a standardized way. Mediactive.com will be part of this.

When you do make a mistake, you should obviously correct it. How to make corrections online is a new genre in itself. Here are several possibilities, in my order of preference:

- For significant errors and updates, correct in context, with a note at the top or the bottom of the piece explaining what has been changed, and why.

- For minor errors, such as a misspelled word, use the "~~strike~~" HTML tag to visibly put a line through the errant material — ~~like this~~—and then add the correct word or words.

- Correct in place and, in a note on the item, link to a corrections page that explains what happened.

The one kind of correction I never advise is the one too often used: an in-place fix with no indication that anything was ever wrong in the first place. Again, remember that mistakes happen, but acting honorably should always be the first order of business.

3. Be Fair and Civil

Fairness is a broader concept than accuracy or thoroughness. It encompasses several related notions:

- Even if you are coming at something from a specific bias or world view, you can be fair to those who disagree with you by incorporating their views into your own work, even if simply to explain why you're right and they're wrong.

- Recognize that you can't be perfectly fair, and that people will hear what you've said through the prisms of their own world views. It's still worth trying.

- You can extend the principle of fairness by inviting others to join the conversation after publication.

- You can stress civility, moreover, as the guiding principle for the conversation.

Why bother, especially if you don't feel others are likely to reciprocate?

First, it's just the the right way to do things. You want other people to deal with you in a fair way, especially when someone is criticizing what you've said or done. Do the same for them, and maybe they will take a similar approach even if they haven't before.

Second, it pays back tactically in audience trust. The people who read or hear your work will feel cheated if you slant the facts or present opposing opinions disingenuously. Your work will be suspect once they realize what you've done—and many eventually will.

How can you be fair? Beyond the Golden Rule notion of treating people as you'd want to be treated, you can ensure that you offer a place for people to reply to what you (and your commenters) have posted. You can insist on civility both in your work and in the comments.

My rule when hosting an online community is that participants will be civil with each other even if we disagree on the issues. This can break down when someone joins a conversation under false pretenses. These can include some obvious behaviors, and others that are more subtle. Here are examples of people to watch out for:

- Someone who is paid by some industry group or has an interest in its success, but who chimes in with opinions about matters of direct concern to the industry without revealing that connection or bias.

- Someone with ideological beliefs that influence his or her position in ways that go beyond a consideration of the facts and issues directly relevant to the position, but who presents the opinion as just the result of reasoning.

- Someone who has a history of unethically (perhaps even illegally) abusing the system in which he or she is participating for personal gain.

It's important to expose the connections, if you detect them, while taking care that the exposé is not an *ad hominem* attack. Creating and sustaining a healthy online community is hard work, as I'll discuss in the next chapter, but it's essential.

Another essential way to be fair is to use links. Point to a variety of material other than your own, to support what you've said and to offer varying perspectives.

Most of all, fairness requires that you listen carefully to what people are saying. Journalism is evolving from a lecture to a conversation we can all be part of, and the first rule of good conversation is to listen.

4. Think Independently

This is similar to the principle described Chapter 2 of opening your mind. It can cover many habits, but independence of thought may be the most important. Creators of media, not just consumers, need to venture beyond their personal comfort zones.

Professional journalists claim independence. They are typically forbidden to have direct or indirect financial conflicts of interest. But conflicts of interest are not always so easy to define. Many prominent Washington journalists, for example, are so blatantly beholden to their sources, and to access to those sources, that they are not independent in any real way, and their journalism reflects it.

Jay Rosen calls out another non-independent frame of mind among the top journalists, particularly in Washington, referring to it as the "Church of the Savvy." According to Rosen, these journalists see themselves as having no ideology but actually share a profoundly deep one:

> Savviness! Deep down, that's what reporters want to believe in and actually do believe in—their own savviness and the savviness of certain others (including [political] operators like Karl Rove). In politics, they believe, it's better to be savvy than it is to be honest or correct on the facts. It's better to be savvy than it is to be just, good, fair, decent, strictly lawful, civilized, sincere or humane.

> Savviness is what journalists admire in others. Savvy is what they themselves dearly wish to be. (And to be unsavvy is far worse than being wrong.) Savviness—that quality of being shrewd, practical, well-informed, perceptive, ironic, "with it,"

and unsentimental in all things political—is, in a sense, their professional religion. They make a cult of it.

Yet aren't we all part of a similar cult in our own lives, or sometimes tempted to be? It's certainly more comfortable to hang out with people who share our own world views, and to seek them out when we're looking for more information. Being independent as a questioner and pursuer of what's actually happening—and I don't care here whether you're paid to be a reporter or not—can get in the way of comfort.

Independent thinking has many facets. Listening, of course, is the best way to start. But you can and should relentlessly question your own conclusions after listening. It's not enough to incorporate the views of opponents into what you write; if what they tell you is persuasive, you have to consider shifting your conclusion, too.

Whether you're a blogger or a paid journalist, independence isn't likely to stretch so far as revealing your employer's dirty laundry or even your own dissatisfaction with what the enterprise is doing. That said, loyalty has its limits; I'd like to think I'd speak out if an employer acted in grossly unethical ways, though I'd probably quit first. In general, however, we should expect that criticism of this kind is normally done in person, behind a closed door. An organization decides its own level of public disclosures, and some internal criticism—especially the kind that might be fodder for a plaintiff's lawyer—is unlikely to see sunlight.

This brings us to the truly new principle: embracing much more openness than ever before.

5. Be Transparent

Transparency is essential not just for citizen journalists and other new media creators, but also for those in traditional media. The kind and extent of transparency may differ. For example, bloggers should explicitly reveal their biases. Big Media employees may have pledged individually not to have conflicts of interest, but that doesn't mean they work without bias. They too should help their audiences understand what they do, and why.

Transparency in the traditional ranks has scarcely existed for most of the past century. While journalists are more publicly open than many other industries in at least some ways, there's a notable hypocrisy quotient. As any of us, professional or not, demand answers from others, we should look in the mirror and ask some of the same questions.

The transparency question boils down to something that may sound counterintuitive but is actually logical: *If you do an honest job as well as you can, greater transparency will lead your audience to trust you more even while they may believe you less.* That is, they'll understand better why it's impossible to get everything right all the time.

Transparency takes several forms. I strongly believe that news organizations have a duty to explain to their audiences how they do their journalism, and why. They could take a page from the newcomers, such as bloggers, the best of whom are much more open on this; their world views and motivations are typically crystal clear. And their audiences, even people who disagree with those world views, can refract their own understanding of the topics through those lenses.

The response I get when I say these things is typically along these lines: If journalists say what they think, they'll call their objectivity into question. Well, I don't believe in objectivity in the first place. And the public already perceives journalists to be biased, which of course they are—though I don't believe this is the same as being unethical.

Bloggers, through their own relentless critiques, have also helped foster transparency in traditional media. However unfair bloggers' criticism may often be, it has been a valuable addition to the media-criticism sphere.

Not all bloggers are adequately transparent. Some, to be sure, do reveal their biases, offering readers a way to consider the writers' world views when evaluating their credibility. But a distinctly disturbing trend in some blog circles is the undisclosed or poorly disclosed conflict of interest. Pay-per-post schemes are high on the list of activities that deserve readers' condemnation; they also deserve a smaller audience.

As noted earlier, these principles aren't the beginning or ending of what trusted media creators should embrace. But if we use them, we're moving in the right direction.

Now let's dig a little deeper into transparency, or being open about what you do and who you are. As I've noted, it's an essential component of being trusted. Some of what's ahead refers to traditional media, but that context is useful for all of us, no matter what media we create in any format.

World Views

I wish that U.S. news organizations would drop the pretense of being impartial and of having no world view. There's no conflict between having a world view and doing great journalism.

When I go to London I buy *The Guardian* and *The Telegraph*. Both do excellent journalism. *The Guardian* covers the world from a slightly left-of-center standpoint, and *The Telegraph* from a slightly right-of-center stance. I read both and figure I'm triangulating on the essence of (British establishment) reality. Even if I read just one, the paper's overt frame of reference gives me a better way of understanding what's happening than if it pretended to be impartial. And—crucially—both newspapers run articles (and lots of op-eds) that either directly challenge their editors' and proprietors' world views or, more routinely, include facts and context that run contrary to what those individuals might wish was true. Journalism's independence of thought means, in particular, being willing or even eager to learn why your core assumptions could be wrong.

Contrast this with the *Washington Post*'s record. This newspaper had a vividly obvious world view during the run-up to the Iraq War: pro-administration and pro-war. The view was reflected principally in the fact that the little journalism it did questioning the premise for invading Iraq rarely, if ever, made the front page, in contrast to the relentless parroting of war-mongering from Bush administration insiders. Even *Post* journalists admitted as much, though not in those words. I'm guessing that the newspaper's editors, who are as good as anyone else in the field, would have done a better job of covering the opposing facts and views if the paper's world view had been stated as a matter of policy, partly because the best journalists enjoy challenging conventional wisdom, even when it's from their own bosses.

Sidebar: Consumer Reports' Integrity in Action

Consumer Reports is a publication that works hard to get things right. But its February 2007 issue ran a dramatically wrong review of children's car seats—due to poor testing methods—and seriously jeopardized the trust it had won from its readers.

The organization's recognition of the problem was the best demonstration I've seen of a) owning up to one's mistakes, b) figuring out what went wrong, c) explaining what happened and d) putting into place policies to prevent such messes in the future.

And it was all done in a public way, with a systematic transparency that's exceedingly rare in journalism.

Soon after the article, which reported that many car seats failed the magazine's tests, came under challenge, it became clear that the tests themselves were flawed. The response from the magazine to its readers and the world was quick: It issued a retraction.

I subscribe to the CR online site. I got an email, and a friend who gets the paper version got the same <u>letter</u> via postal mail, from <u>Jim Guest</u>, president of <u>Consumers Union</u>, the title's parent. He apologized, sincerely. He explained what he knew so far about the error, apparently caused by an outside lab's tests. He announced a further investigation. And he promised extraordinary efforts not to let it occur again.

In March 2007, the very next issue, CR posted a detailed report (which also ran online) titled "<u>How our car seat tests went wrong</u>." The "series of misjudgments" described in the piece is remarkable. It was especially worrisome given the publication's record. I don't rely on CR for everything I buy, but I've learned to trust its overall judgment on relatively uncomplicated consumer goods such as kitchen appliances, where I'm unlikely to spend much time on my own extra research. Were I the parent of small children, I might well have included car seats in that category.

The report explained everything about the tests in clear and unsparing language. It included justifiably angry comments from a car seat manufacturer and from outside critics. It was self-criticism of the sort one almost never sees from a journalistic organization, blogger or other media creator of any kind.

CR also posted a story called "<u>Learning from our mistake</u>," a description of what it would do to avoid similar catastrophes in the future. Among other things, it announced that the publication planned to bring outside experts into the process when creating complicated testing procedures (and already does that to a degree), to fix the way it works with outside labs and to look much harder "when our findings are unusual."

The last of those should have been second nature to the journalists and scientists at CR. After all, it's famous for telling readers that when something seems too good to be true, it probably isn't. In this case—with all those car seats failing the test—perhaps it was too bad to be true.

The magazine might consider opening its testing procedures in other ways. For example, it could create videos of the tests as they're being conducted and post them online. Bring in the designated experts, by all means, but maybe some readers who are experts in their own way might spot something useful, such as an omission in the testing procedure or a valuable way to improve it.

Bloggers, Come Clean

One of the most entertaining blogs in the tech field has been the "<u>Fake Steve Jobs</u>" commentary by author and magazine writer <u>Daniel</u>

Lyons. His identity wasn't known publicly during the blog's early days. When it was finally revealed, a number of people recalled something else Lyons had written. As <u>Anil Dash</u> wrote on his blog in a posting called "Hypocrite or New Believer?":

> Daniel Lyons, author of the heretofore-anonymous Fake Steve Jobs blog, which comments extensively on companies in the technology industry, was also the author of Forbes' November 2005 cover story "Attack of the Blogs", a 3000-word screed vilifying anonymous bloggers who comment on companies in the technology industry.
>
> In 2005, I spoke to Lyons for the article, though the comments I made about both the efforts that have been made to encourage accountability in the blogopshere, as well as the many positive benefits that businesses have accrued from blogging, were omitted from the story. My initial temptation was to mark Lyons as a hypocrite. Upon reflection, it seems there's a more profound lesson: The benefits of blogging for one's career or business are so profound that they were even able to persuade a dedicated detractor.

I'm going with hypocrisy. (I say that with this caveat: Lyons's Fake Steve Jobs remains a terrific feature, often better in my view than his work at *Forbes* and, as of this writing, *Newsweek*.)

Lyons's decision to admit who he was—after he was <u>outed</u> by a reporter who did sufficient legwork—was a victory for transparency in a sphere that is often more transparent than traditional media, but not always.

The online world is rife with conflicts of interest stemming from non-transparency. On blogs and many other sites where conversation among the audience is part of the mix, we often encounter so-called "sock puppets"—people posting under pseudonyms instead of their real names, and either promoting their own work or denigrating their opponents, sometimes in the crudest ways. As with people engaging in the often odious practice called "buzz marketing" —paid or otherwise rewarded to talk up products without revealing that they're being compensated — it's widely believed that the people getting caught are a small percentage of the ones doing it.

Enforced Online Transparency

The Federal Trade Commission, with laudable goals, issued a <u>document</u> in late 2009 aimed at better disclosure, with penalties of up to

$11,000 in fines for violations. Basically, the FTC was saying that if you have a "material connection" to a product or service you're praising, you are an endorser who must disclose that connection.

Sounds good, doesn't it? But when you read the FTC's ruling you get the sense of a government-gone-wild travesty. The system is unworkable in practice, which is bad enough. Worse, the rules are worryingly vague and wide-ranging. Worse yet, they give traditional print and broadcast journalists a pass while applying harsh regulations to bloggers (and others using conversational media of various kinds). Worst, and most important, they are, in the end, an attack on markets and free speech, based on a 20th century notion of media and advertising that simply doesn't map to the new era.

The advertising of the past was a one-to-many system. Call it broadcasting. The Internet is a many-to-many system. Call that conversation. They are not the same.

The commission took pains in the uproar that followed the guidelines' release to insist that no one planned to go after individual bloggers. Rather, the targets would be slippery marketers who were trying to pull wool over the eyes of consumers. This clarification was only modestly reassuring. Plans change, and the rules were written with such deliberate vagueness that I predict it's only a matter of time before the FTC does begin chasing after individuals it deems problematic.

The FTC's first enforcement action was heartening, in a way, as it seemed to show a keen sense of how such regulations should be used. The commission settled a case with a California PR firm whose employees had posted glowing reviews of clients' games in Apple's online store without disclosing they were being paid for this. The firm, Reverb Communications, agreed to remove what amounted to advertisements and not do it again, though as usual in these cases it didn't admit (or deny) doing anything wrong.

If these are the kinds of things the FTC will go after, we'll be okay. I continue to worry, however, that the agency could go further and damage online speech. We should all loathe the odious practice of using bloggers and other online conversationalists as commercial sock puppets in a deceptive online word-of-mouth operation. And we can all agree that disclosures are always better than hiding one's affiliation with a company.

We already have laws against fraud. Let's enforce those—first against the serious fraudsters, who keep getting away with it—before we even consider harsh regulations on speech.

Can Honor Prevail?

A few years ago, when I was working on my <u>Bayosphere</u> local media startup, my co-founder, <u>Michael Goff</u>, and I wondered how we could do more than simply encourage Bayosphere's citizen journalists to operate according to the best principles of journalism in their posts and comments. We came up with an idea that failed, like the overall site, but I still believe it had some merit.

The notion, which we called "Honor Tags," was meant to be a system by which site participants could label themselves as "journalists," "advocates," or "neither," with clear definitions for the first two roles. We hoped to persuade people to assess themselves and their own work, and we had in mind a second-level system by which others in the community could judge whether the tags were accurate. The idea was modestly praised by some as a potentially valuable system, and mercilessly ridiculed by others as utopian nuttiness.

The key value we hoped to instill, however, has not faded at all. If honor isn't a part of how we do our work, we'll forfeit any reason to be trusted.

This is why I sometimes despair about professional journalists' rampant violations of their own standards at the media organizations I respect the most, such as the *New York Times*, where anonymous sources still get too-free reign. Yet it's also why I nod with satisfaction when I see a news operation work harder to explain itself and its work, and why I grin at the many experiments aimed at adding transparency and accountability—elements of honor—to journalism at all levels.

News providers of all stripes can announce their standards. If you're one of them, you should do so and live up to them, admitting publicly when you fail. In the end, community members, doing commerce in the fabled marketplace of ideas, will enforce them.

Chapter 6

Tools and Tactics for Trusted Creators

The tools of digital media creation are becoming ubiquitous, certainly in the developed world and increasingly on a global scale as well. They encompass such a wide variety of technologies and methods that I could spend this entire volume just talking about the ones you can use right now—and by the time you finished reading, there would be new ones.

So, in this chapter we'll look in a high-level way at how to make your own media. As always, we'll extend and amplify at mediactive.com.

It's especially useful to know the most widely used tools and techniques and to understand why people are so excited about some of the emerging ones. Our teenagers are using most of these tools already, especially social networks and mobile texting, and in many families younger children are being immersed in electronic gadgets of all kinds. (Like all tools, digital ones can be used for good or bad purposes, and with positive and negative consequences for the user; I'll address that in another chapter.) And if you're reading this book, chances are you're using at least some media creation tools.

I've arranged this chapter's sections in order from the most basic to the more complex—that is, starting with the ones you're most likely to be using already and moving along a path to the tools and techniques that demand more expertise.

There's no way to list, much less discuss, all of the available technologies and services. I'm focusing here on a few that strike me as the main ones where people are already participating and contributing in trusted ways, including several that require a more serious commitment of your time.

None of these is all that difficult, but I recognize that everyone has a personal limit. So when you reach yours, as you read on, it's fine to stop there and continue to the next chapter. If you do that, I hope you'll come back sometime and read what you've skipped.

Simple Text: Mail Lists and Discussion Groups

In this day of video, audio, mashups and all kinds of advanced media forms, we sometimes forget the value of plain old text. That can be a mistake, because text is easy to take in and, for most people, easier to create than linear media like videos.

You don't even have to be a blogger to use text to great effect in communities of all kinds. Even a simple email list can be a great way to keep people in touch, and to pass around valuable information. If you can pull people to your blog, it's great for disseminating ideas, but often you'll get more attention by posting a brief message to an appropriate mailing list already frequented by the people you want to reach.

There are thousands and thousands of mail lists, message boards and other kinds of systems of this sort. They exist for conversation and to provide information, and they can be amazingly valuable. They're designed for easy participation. Some allow anonymous posting; others require a sign-up with a valid email address in order to deter bad behavior. Although some go even further and require each mail to be checked by a moderator, this kind of gatekeeping is rarely used anymore because it holds up discussion.

Of course, it's fine to lurk in the background, reading without posting; in fact, a general rule on forums is that you should read for at least a couple of days before you add your voice, to get a sense of the culture and what's acceptable to post. Ultimately, you'll get the most out of these forums by joining in. The more you know about a topic, the more you can help others understand it, too. No matter who you are, you know more than enough about *something* to be a valuable participant.

Forums and mail lists are also simple to create yourself. It's especially easy at big Internet sites like Google Groups and Yahoo! Groups. If you don't already have an account, just create one. Then create a group, and you're off to the races.

The limits of running a group or mail list via Google or Yahoo! become fairly obvious once you've spent enough time there. You can move up to more sophisticated forum software—there are literally dozens of products and services to choose from—but going this route does add several layers of complexity.

I've been on mail lists and forums of various kinds for years. Some are just entertaining, but others have serious value as community information providers. For example, our former neighborhood in a northern-California city—a few square blocks with several hundred homes—was served by a community website that offered basic information about the area. But the more valuable online information source was a Yahoo! Groups message board where residents discussed local news. One day, someone posted a message saying that the tap water had gotten cloudy. Someone else noticed the same thing. Not too many hours later, we found out the scoop: According to a resident who called the city utilities department, repairs to the system were causing the cloudiness, but it was not at all dangerous to anyone's health; the poster of this message also linked to a page on the city's website explaining the situation.

This incident was not nearly important enough to have been of interest to the (formerly) big daily newspaper in Silicon Valley, my old employer. As far as I know it didn't even make the weekly serving our town. But it was real, serious news in our neighborhood, as were other messages over the years letting folks know about local break-ins and vandalism.*

Social Networks: Facebook and More

In mid-2010, Facebook announced it had reached an amazing milestone: 500 million signups worldwide. You may well be one of them. Almost without exception, my students are. So am I.

I should say at the outset that while I have immense respect for the brilliance of the Facebook founder and team, I'm not a huge fan of Facebook itself, for reasons I'll explain in more detail later in the book; suffice it to say, for now, that I don't like Facebook's ever-morphing privacy policies and I especially worry that it's creating a walled garden that diminishes the rest of the online world. But it's hugely popular, in part because it does what it does so seamlessly and, for users, in a helpful way. Whatever I think of the service, it's the preeminent social network—MySpace and LinkedIn are a considerable distance behind in sheer numbers—and it's developed into an impressive ecosystem that clearly has staying power.

To create an ecosystem, Facebook encouraged third parties to use its software platform to create other products and services within the Facebook service itself: everything from posting pictures to sharing travel

---

*Information created at the "hyper-local" level, as some call the geography, takes a contrarian twist from the old adage, "It's not news when dog bites man, but it is news when man bites dog." That's true enough if the news provider is a big-city paper or TV station. But "dog bites man" is definitely news if it happens on your street, more so if the dog bit your next-door neighbor—and especially if it was your dog.

plans to playing online games, and on and on. You can spend a lot of time inside Facebook and get a lot out of the experiences.

The updating mechanism at services of this kind, called a "wall" at Facebook, is in its own way a news service, where the news and observations come from people you know or have "friended" there. The value of what you read (and see in photos and videos) depends, of course, on how useful or entertaining you find what others post. But purely for social interaction, there's a lot to be said for using social networks as a way to stay in touch.

Should you "friend" everyone who asks? That is, should you agree to share your private information with other people more or less indiscriminately? Definitely not. Most people online, as in the physical world, are good. But enough are not that you should be at least somewhat cautious in how you approach social networks.

We need to take privacy issues extremely seriously. After Facebook made what I considered a dramatic change in its policies, I decided to quit and start over, as I'll explain in Chapter 9. And as I'll also discuss in the same chapter, privacy is at the core of what I hope will be changing customs in an always-connected age.

Again, while the rise of Facebook has been meteoric, and well-earned, it's hardly the only social network. MySpace has a huge number of users, and while it no longer has its former cachet it remains highly popular, especially when used for its primary purpose: music discovery and promotion. I don't visit it much, but researcher danah boyd has observed that MySpace still is one of the most widely used networks, second only to Facebook.

I use LinkedIn for much of my social-networking interaction. It's aimed at the business community, but it's a terrific network for finding people who share your vocational or professional interests. I tell my students, nearly all of whom have Facebook accounts, that they should have LinkedIn accounts when they head out into the job market. (I and many others have had great success using LinkedIn to recruit new colleagues.)

You can create your own social network without all that much difficulty, too. Ning.com does this brilliantly, with many of the best features of the big networks available out of the virtual box. I've used Ning for university classes, to keep students informed of events in class, and found one of its best features to be the ability to make the network entirely private among its members, invisible to the outside world. (As we'll discuss later, though, it's always best to assume that anything you create online for someone else—anyone else—to look at may someday escape out to the rest of the world.) Ning started off as a free service. It now charges, but I still recommend it highly.

Even blogging platforms, discussed in the next section, are becoming more like social networks. For example, the people behind WordPress have created BuddyPress, an add-on that brings social networking capabilities to the blogging system. It's what I'm using now for classes, and while it doesn't offer all the bells and whistles (yet) of other social networks, it works just fine for our purposes, even allowing us to keep things private.

Blogging

A blog is a series of updates in reverse chronological order, with the newest material at the top. That's it. Simple, no?

Yet blogging is a term that encompasses any number of forms; it can be turned to a variety of purposes, as millions of people around the globe have discovered. Blogging has become one of the most preferred ways for people to post news, opinions and, yes, even what they've had for breakfast as they write from their basements in their pajamas—the latter a capsule description of the way some people like to deride citizen media.

Blogging providers and services abound. The "big 3" services for individuals are:

Blogger: a free hosting service owned by Google that's probably the least flexible of the pack but also probably the simplest to use. Google let Blogger languish for a time, but it has been improving the service lately.

WordPress: currently my blogging software of choice. WordPress has both hosted (free and paid) and self-serve options where you install the software on a computer owned by you or your Web hosting service. It also has a large variety of "plug-ins" that let you extend and customize what you can post and how people can view and use it.

TypePad: a mostly paid hosting service from Movable Type, a company that has focused more and more on the business market.

Posterous: aimed at folks who prefer visuals and short updates to lots of text. Along with a similar service called Tumblr, it's one of the faster-growing sites in the genre.

The main thing to understand about any of these blogging services is their convenience. You can create a blog in about five minutes, and later you can make it pretty much as simple or elaborate as you want.

If you have a passion for something, blogging is a natural outlet. The best bloggers have several things in common:

- They write with a genuine, conversational human voice, more like a letter to a friend than formal journalism. A blog is not a press release machine, or at least shouldn't be.

- They invite conversation. This trait isn't universal: Some extremely popular blogs don't allow comments, for reasons that seem appropriate to the people who run those sites. But I strongly advise that you not just allow comments, but encourage them.

- They link out to other sources. They don't just tell what the author knows or thinks, but point readers to useful material from others as well.

Should you write infrequent but long posts, or frequent but pithy ones, or something in between? My answer is: Yes. Do whatever you feel is best, not what someone prescribes. (If you want to get lots of traffic, or visits from other people, more frequent updates are generally a good idea.)

For years and years, the question has kept coming up: Is blogging journalism? We may as well ask whether writing on paper is journalism. The answer, of course, is that most blogging is not journalism, but some blogging is. In short, as blogging pioneer (among many other accomplishments) Dave Winer has pointed out, blogs are tools to be used in any number of different ways. Let's agree never to ask this question again, okay?

Twitter (Microblogging)

The traditional media pick a Big New Thing in Technology all the time, and in 2009 it was Twitter. This time, the traditional media got it right.

Twitter is a "microblogging" service that lets you post messages of up to 140 characters in length, called "tweets." That's not as short as a typical newspaper headline, but it's not long enough for more than a basic thought.

Yet the very limitation of Twitter—combined with absolutely brilliant positioning by the company—has turned it into what has aptly been termed the "nervous system of the Web." The flow of information on the service is diverse, of course, given the millions of users; but it's also useful, not just entertaining.

Twitter users soon find that almost every event they care about—if they are following the right people—is first mentioned in the "tweetstream." Search engines aren't as good at capturing real-time information flow, though they're getting better at it (and increasingly they include Twitter in their own results.) Of course, the value of this stream of data depends as well on whether you're paying close attention; it's easy to miss things that scroll by. With third-party Twitter-management software, discussed briefly below, you can set up searches to keep track of things you care about.

I use Twitter both as a creator and a reader; it's an essential part of my daily media. I use it as an alert system to get tips and early warnings, and to keep an eye on what people I respect think is important. I follow the "Tweets" (Twitter postings) of about 350 people and organizations. I've selected and organized them carefully, looking for rich information from the relative few rather than a fire hose from the many. Many of the people I follow are involved in the media. I post frequently as well, and as of this writing have about 11,000 followers—a decent number, but not remotely in the ballpark of the most avidly followed people or services.

The main reason Twitter has become so popular is that the people behind it—including Evan Williams, co-founder of Blogger (see a pattern?)—have made the service the center of an ecosystem. They've made it easy for other people to build applications and services on the tweets of the millions of Twitter users, in all kinds of ways.* Third-party applications that manage your Twitter stream are invaluable for organizing the people you follow and creating searches that you can check from time to time.

If you have a blog, you can use Twitter to build the audience by tweeting to point to blog postings you think are particularly interesting. I don't recommend tweeting about every blog post, because your Twitter followers may well grow tired of this kind of self-promotion when they can just as easily get an RSS feed from your blog.

In general, the best newsworthy Tweets contain hyperlinks to something else. When someone I follow because I like her work suggests I look at something related to her expertise and makes it sound interesting in her brief description, I tend to click through and check it out. I can't overstate the value of Twitter when used in this manner.

---

* I'm an investor in one of the third-party companies creating software for Twitter users, called Seesmic. By some reckonings, the most popular Twitter client application is TweetDeck. Most are free or low-cost, so try them until you find one *you* like.

Because of the 140-character limit, Twitter has spurred the use of URL-shortening services such as bit.ly and is.gd, which shorten the Web addresses you submit to a Twitter-appropriate lengths. However, the use of these services has raised a number of questions, including the permanence of the links and how search engines will handle valuable links that actually send you to something else, as well as security questions.

Audio: Podcasts and More

We are, in some ways, what we listen to. I love music, and I love the spoken word.

We're in the early days of an audio revolution. Other digital media are also undergoing rapid change, but audio has a special nature of its own.

Whether you listen to the radio or podcasts or audio of other kinds, there is a special quality to listening. You are forced, in a good way, to use your imagination. When I listen to a news program on National Public Radio I am filling in gaps in my mind, visualizing the parts I'm not seeing.

Podcasting is the most important of the emerging audio methods, at least in the context of news and information. The easiest way to think of podcasts is as audio blogs: episodic, available over the Internet via syndication, and displaying the newest postings first. (I'd bet that most people find new podcasts through searches and links from other sites, however.)

As with blogs, the variety of podcasts is enormous. The most popular podcasting (and music) delivery system is Apple's iTunes store, but you can find podcasts in many other ways as well. Also as with with blogs, you can host your audio files yourself, or you can find services that will host them on their computers (something I recommend for both audio and video).

The software tools you need to create good podcasts come with every new desktop or laptop computer. Apple's GarageBand software has podcast-specific features, for example. There's also a huge amount of free or low-cost software available online, if you decide to get more sophisticated about your recordings.

To join the audio movement, you should have a decent headset with a microphone for recording and playback at home or in the office. If you're interviewing people in the field, you should consider buying a decent external microphone and audio recorder, although modern digital cameras usually let you record audio and video, and today's smart phones can do what you need if you don't mind not-so-great audio and picture quality.

Although an audio news show or segment—compiled material that is edited before distribution—is considerably more complex to create than most blog posts, you don't have to be an audio or news-radio pro to create a useful podcast. Sometimes a recording of a conversation is all you need: Imagine talk radio, democratized. One of the most interesting podcast series around is called "Rebooting the News"; it was originated by blog pioneer Dave Winer and New York University journalism professor Jay Rosen (both friends of mine), who ruminate—often with guests, including me on one occasion—on the state of news. Their weekly series, far from getting stale, has only grown more interesting over time.

Visual: Photos and Videos

Sooner or later—though more quickly in the developed world—almost everyone will be walking around with a camera capable of recording both still photos and video—the one in his or her mobile phone. It's already getting difficult to buy a phone that doesn't at least take photos, and video recording capabilities are becoming more common, too. Meanwhile, digital still and video cameras continue to sell by the millions, and their capabilities improve at the steady pace we've come to expect from modern digital technology.

What kind of equipment should you use? I tend to agree with Chase Jarvis, who says "the best camera is the one that's with you"—he's written a book and iPhone app, and created an online community, to reinforce this point. Without the camera, there's no picture or video.

If you take lots of pictures, you may well want to share some or all of them with others, not just keep them on your own computer. If so, look at online services such as Flickr, a Yahoo! operation that takes in some 750 photos every second. If you're going to be a heavy user of Flickr and other such services, you'll need to consider signing up for a paid account that gives you more storage and upload capacity.

If it's 10 times harder to create an excellent audio report than a piece of text, it may be another 10 times harder, or at least more time-consuming, to create an excellent video. But even here, the ease of production is rapidly improving, and younger people who have grown up with video as part of their routine media toolkits are showing older folks (like me) new tricks.

A video doesn't have to be elaborate or fancy, though. I tend to create videos for two main purposes: interviews and scene-setting. Neither is a full-blown production. Interviews are simple: Just set up a camera (and an external microphone, if you have one), and have at it. By scene-setting I mean using the video as a window into your subject. Suppose you're interviewing a businessperson for a blog posting. You can shoot a quick video of his or her office, so your own audience can easily visualize the place you visited. This takes no special shooting or editing skills, but still has real value.

What should you do with the videos? Most people store them on someone else's site, commonly YouTube. There are good reasons to do this: notably, the ease of uploading and the willingness of Google, which owns YouTube, to cover the considerable costs of making these files available on the Internet. (Do keep a backup copy of everything you create, though!) YouTube is so popular that as of November 2010 people were uploading 35 hours of video per minute.

Of course, as with social networks and other tools, the most popular sites are not the only ones around. I don't necessarily recommend YouTube for videos, because it still hasn't given users an easy way to make videos available under the Creative Commons copyright license, which encourages wider sharing of digital material. I do recommend Blip.TV for that purpose; the service specifically creates a default setting for Creative Commons licensing. (Flickr also has a Creative Commons option, one reason I still recommend it.)

Mashups, APIs, Tagging and More

Stop reading for a second if you're holding the printed edition of this book. Fire up your Web browser and look at the "Tunisian Prison Map" online at http://www.nawaat.org/tunisianprisonersmap. Click on any of the pointers in the map, and it will take you deeper into a repository of information about Tunisia's human rights abuses. The map's lead creator, Sami Ben Gharbia, pulled data from a variety of sources and used Google Maps to help illustrate what he found. It's brilliant work, and in a good cause.

The Tunisian map is an example of a mashup—a combination of data and Web services that could not have existed before the Web 2.0 era. It relies on a technology called the Application Programming Interface (API). APIs are used to make connections between different websites and services, by allowing one to interoperate with others. The electrical socket in a wall is, in effect, an API to devices that use electricity.

You don't have to have a lot of experience with technology to create your own mashup. Google Maps and its competitors let you put virtual pins on maps and then annotate them with your own information. Some news organizations have done something similar; for example, the *Bakersfield Californian* newspaper put up a map and asked readers to pinpoint the locations of potholes in the city streets. You could do the same in your own neighborhood (let your city government officials know, because they're the ones who can get the holes filled!). Even easier for this purpose than Google Maps for beginners is CitySourced.com, which is specifically aimed at improving local services.

Mashups are fundamentally about data, but some of the best ones are also about visualizing that data. Numbers, dates and the like don't tell you much by themselves, but when you combine them with visual techniques they start to sing a tune we can all understand. One of my favorites in this genre is a video timeline of Wal-Mart deployments across the continental U.S., with dots on the map starting in a small city in Arkansas and ultimately spreading across the nation in a view that is unpleasantly reminiscent of an epidemic.

The Web is loaded with excellent resources for creating mashups. We have a list on the Mediactive site, but I recommend starting at a site called, logically, Programmable Web, which offers a great "how to" on creating your own mashup. It starts with "Pick a subject" and goes into detail from there.

Content-Management Systems

What if your Blogger.com or WordPress.com blog isn't enough? What if you want to create a more sophisticated information site or service, offering community features and a variety of bells and whistles not available in typical blog software?

You may have just crossed over into the CMS zone.

CMS stands for *content-management system*, a term that describes a variety of software and Web services that do what the name suggests: management of various kinds of content. There's a CMS behind every major news site. (To be clear, WordPress and other blog platforms are content-management systems, too; I've separated them here because what follows ups the ante on flexibility, as well as complexity. But I'm increasingly impressed with how powerful WordPress has become even in this category.)

Content-management systems typically combine two major components. The first is a database: usually a free (open source) package called MySQL. That's where everything you create—postings, comments, pictures, etc.—resides. The CMS itself is software that: a) helps you create the material that goes into the database; b) pulls data out of that database to create Web pages for display on computer screens, phones and other devices; and c) helps you manage your website.

As noted, hosted blogging software is a form of CMS, too: It just manages the content in a few specific ways, giving you less flexibility in return for greater ease of use (and ease of management for the company hosting the blogs).

Setting up your own CMS is not trivial. Unless you are technically adept, you should find a Web hosting company that will help you create your CMS, or find a partner who knows how, or even hire someone to do it for you, or both. Trust me on this.

You can choose among literally hundreds of CMS packages. Check the Mediactive website for a list of sites that can help you find and use a system that will fit your needs. Two systems of note are:

Drupal: Probably the best known open-source (free to download, use and modify), multi-purpose CMS. (Joomla!, another CMS of this genre, has a large and passionate following as well; in fact, it's more popular than Drupal in some places.) Drupal is a highly modular system: you can plug in all kinds of add-ons to tweak and customize your site. It has a large community of users and developers, a big plus if you're going to be making significant changes to the core features (you almost certainly will). But Drupal can also be an extremely frustrating system, partly due to that very flexibility. My own relationship with Drupal is very much in the love-hate category. You'll find Drupal at http://drupal.org.

MediaWiki: We discussed Wikipedia in an earlier chapter. Did you know that the software used to run the site is freely available? It's also getting more powerful all the time. The MediaWiki.org site, which hosts the software of the same name, is itself a Wiki, of course, and it offers downloads and thorough instructions on how to use it. Just because it's a Wiki doesn't mean you have to let anyone edit any page; you can allow only certain people to make changes.

Mobile, the Emerging Frontier

My current mobile phone is called the "Nexus One," and it's way, way more than just a phone. It's a mobile computing device, combining phone, camera, camcorder, GPS location, Web and multimedia services, and lots more.

It's far from the only option out there, of course. Apple's iPhone has been a huge hit, as has its iPad tablet computer, and other manufacturers offer highly capable "smart phones" as well. Mobile computing using these devices is a huge part of our future.

The explosion of highly sophisticated mobile devices is still in a relative infancy. Even at this early stage, however, the mobile revolution has changed pretty much everything we knew about our relationship to technology. The latest mobile devices have these characteristics:

- They're always connected (in theory, at any rate). You can communicate wherever you are, in a variety of ways, including via text, audio, photo, video and more.

- They know where they are. Modern devices have built-in GPS, or global positioning, to within a few meters. Some also have compasses, so they know what direction their cameras are facing. If you're like me, the single most valuable mobile application I use is Google Maps.

- They are creating not just the data you designate, but a host of other information that (if you choose) is always attached to what you create. This means, for example, that if you take a picture and send it to, say, Flickr, the photo-sharing service automatically checks to see if there's location information and, if so, puts the picture into a map.

Software developers are off to the races to come up with novel ways to use the capabilities of these devices. One of the most intriguing uses is what's called "augmented reality," in which you use the phone's camera to look at your surroundings, and then have those surroundings annotated with whatever other people have posted online about the area—everything from the location (plus patron reviews) of the local steakhouse to the location of the nearest cardiologist, with turn-by-turn directions to both.

So far, smart phones have been most valuable as devices we use to get information. One of my favorite tests is to scan the bar code of an item in a store and then check, using the device's various capabilities, where else it's for sale in the neighborhood or online, and at what price.

You can easily imagine the journalism potential. For example, it would be easy to map graffiti (or potholes, or just about anything else) in your city, annotated with pictures. My students created a map and photo gallery of local art galleries during a Phoenix "First Friday Art Walk," a monthly event when people from all over the metropolitan area converge on the downtown visual arts scene.

The latest and perhaps most intriguing use of the new mobile devices is combining location awareness with social networking. Not only have Facebook, LinkedIn, Twitter, MySpace and other social systems moved swiftly to these platforms, but a host of new services are emerging as well. Some, such as <u>Foursquare</u> and <u>Gowalla</u>, invite users to announce their locations and then see what's happening in the neighborhood, and who else is there.

By the time this appears in print, of course, we'll have heard about dozens or scores of new mobile devices and applications, each promising (and possibly delivering) more than what came before. We'll keep an eye on them on the Mediactive website, in the context of media creation.

As with social networking on PCs, and with all of the content you create, there are privacy issues attached to mobility—some that are much more troubling than anything we've encountered in the past. I'll discuss this more in Chapter 9.

Terms of Service, Etc.

When you register to use an online service, you are almost always confronted with a checkbox you must click in order to proceed. Almost everyone checks it, but almost no one reads the <u>Terms of Service</u> to which they're agreeing.

My overarching goal in this chapter (and this book as a whole) is to help you jump in and join the journalistic conversation. But you can't ignore the legalities, especially if you're planning to create media that may have a commercial aspect. Some people, including me, refuse to use certain popular sites—or take extra care not to use them for any significant work or play—because of restrictions they impose or how the sites might use the data posted there. I put Facebook into this category.

I strongly suggest that you do read the privacy policies and terms of service on the sites you use. I also hope that Internet services will liberalize their policies toward greater user privacy, freedom and reuse of what people post, such as promoting Creative Commons, a copyright licensing system that reserves only some, not all, rights for the author so that works can be seen and used by the widest possible audience. It's in the best interest of the sites' owners, I believe, to protect privacy and promote openness. That's why I believe they'll move more and more in those directions.

Community

One of the most important roles you'll have in the new media environment is creating and managing community. What you do in a socially mediated world is at least as much about community as what you produce on your own. The conversations you foster online will help people understand what you're doing, and will help you keep them involved.

Until very recently, newspapers and broadcasters have failed miserably at creating community. They've barely even grasped the basics, in part because their traditional one-to-many model fostered institutional arrogance. Luckily, we can learn from people who jumped in early.

Robert Niles, who has created a number of online services including the award-winning ThemeParkInsider.com, says that tomorrow's journalists will need to be community organizers—and that you'll need to understand that the people who pay the bills, not just the audience, comprise one of the communities you'll need to organize and serve. This is true for a one-person effort or a larger one.

"Know what you're doing online," Niles says. "Embrace community organizing; create value for a community... [and] you will find a community that will value you."

According to Niles, the role of a community organizer doesn't just imply taking stands; it almost demands it. At the same time, one should never lose sight of journalistic principles:

> Embrace advocacy, but let it be guided by smart reporting and thoughtful community engagement. That will be what distinguishes your site, and your community, from the many blogs and websites run by people who aren't as capable as reporters, or as effective in community organizing.

You'll find lots of resources online about community creation. We'll list a bunch of them online, but in the end you'll need to recognize that the key is you: If you don't take this seriously, you won't be able to make it work.

Trolls and Breakage

One essential part of community management is preventing the kind of damage that bad folks can cause, and fixing it when they inevitably do. This is about more than keeping your software up to date with security "patches" and other preventive maintenance. It's about the conversation, too.

If you've participated in online conversations in a more-than-casual way, you probably know how quickly they can turn wrong. Scary, ugly wrong.

There's something about speaking anonymously that inspires people to misbehave. They'll say things to each other that they wouldn't dream of saying in person, partly because they're not within physical reach.

In Chapter 11 I'll propose a community user-management system that (as far as I know) doesn't yet exist. It would discriminate—I use that word deliberately—among various kinds of members, giving the most credence to people who use verified real names and are rated highly by other credible members of the community. Even though we don't have an ideal system of this sort, we're not helpless today in the face of the trolls.

Well-meaning people (including me) have suggested honor codes, blogger comment guidelines and all sorts of other non-technical ways to enforces civil behavior. I'm skeptical of anything that we might try to impose on anyone, but I do believe that we, as community hosts, have every right—even a duty—to impose rules inside our own sites. Simply put, I don't invite people into my home and then tolerate them spitting on the living room rug (literally or figuratively). You shouldn't, either. And you should enforce the rules you set.

When I ran a community site in 2005, I consulted several friends about rules of the road for folks who wanted to join the community. They included my friend Lisa Stone and her team at BlogHer.com, who have created a thoughtful set of guidelines; I recommend you start there when coming up with your own. My own site's guidelines borrowed from BlogHer and several other sites. Here's an excerpt:

> In short, we aim here for civility and mutual respect. Beyond that, we encourage robust discussions and debate.
>
> Members may be blocked from the site for vandalism, making personal attacks on other members, publishing others' copyrighted material or for violating the guidelines and comments policy.
>
> Offensive, inflammatory or otherwise inappropriate screen names are not permitted, and the use of these will be prevented through blocking of accounts. Members blocked for having an inappropriate name will be permitted to rejoin under a new name.

We also recognized that the rules weren't the final word, and moreover that we couldn't possibly watch everything. So we added:

Remember, we need your help.

This is a community. If you see material that violates our site rules and guidelines, please contact us.

Please also make suggestions, on our forums or via e-mail, on how we might improve these terms and guidelines.

Feel free to borrow and amend—that's another way the Internet works at its best.

Comment-moderation systems are becoming more sophisticated, and the best community sites police themselves to some degree: The users spot the bad stuff and help the site managers get rid of it. But even the best-run sites have problems dealing with the truly malevolent people. The Web still has its trolls and others who wreck things for sport. This is an arms race that won't end anytime soon, but if the community is on your—and its own—side, you can keep up.

It's More Than Technology

The most important element in your media creation is not the technology. The tools get cheaper and easier to use all the time. There's scarcely any financial barrier to entry.

What matters is you. If you have the skills, or are willing to learn them, you can stand out from the avalanche of information that pours over us every day. If you have the energy to pursue your media creation, you'll get more done than someone who doesn't care as much.

Most of all, if you have the integrity to do things right—to follow the principles that add up to honorable journalism—you can be a creator who makes a difference, whether it's in your neighborhood or, perhaps, on a global scale.

Chapter 7

Owning Your Online Presence

Who are you, anyway? In the digital world, just as in the physical one, you are partly who others say you are.

This is why you need to be at least one—and preferably the most prominent—of the voices talking about you. You can't allow others to define who you are, or control the way you are perceived. This is especially true today for people in the public eye, but the more we do online the more it'll be true for the rest of us, too.

We're moving into new territory here. We've previously discussed the value of joining online conversations. Now I want to recognize that those conversations may, in some respects, be about you and your ideas. You need to know what people may be saying about you or your work. And you need to respond when necessary, especially when you need to clarify or correct what someone has said.

Being public in this increasingly public world means participating. It means recognizing that what you do online influences the way others see you. This goes under many names: reputation, brand, influence and the like. For our purposes I'll call it "brand," but I'm not using the word in a commercial or marketing sense; rather, it's about how you appear to the world beyond your family and closest friends, and what you can do to be seen as you truly are.

In this chapter, we'll discuss why, and how, you should consider becoming what amounts to a publisher in your own right. I can almost see your eyebrows rising as you read this, but don't worry. Remember, this is the Digital Age. You don't have to buy printing presses, or put up big broadcast towers, or employ anyone. Publishing today is what we all do. The word carries historical freight, but it's now an everyday act.

What I'm getting at, however, is a crucial point: To the extent that it's possible to do so, you should control the reference point for people who want to know more about you and your ideas. We'll look at how you can create, own and operate that online touchpoint—call it a home base, above and beyond the blogging or tweeting you might do elsewhere—for who you are, and what you do. As always, look for much more detail about specific tools and techniques at the Mediactive website.

Again, the basics:

1. Whether you create your own media or not, you need to join the conversation when people are talking about you or your work.

2. Creating media and joining conversations will get you only part of the way. You also need to create your own online home base, one that you truly control.

Your Place

If you go to <u>dangillmor.com</u>, you'll find more about me, and by me, than you're likely to care about. The point is, it's all there. I've made that site my personal home base on the Web. You should consider doing something like it.

Why would you want to do this? Because you need to present yourself online on at least one page or site that you control, where others can check you out—I call it a home base here but on my own page I call it my "anchor site." The more we participate in online social life, and the more our offline doings are fodder for what others see, capture and say about us, the more we need to give people a way to read our own take on things, unfiltered.

Please note: I'm absolutely not suggesting that you avoid social networks like Facebook, MySpace, Twitter, Foursquare and any number of other services designed for communication and collaboration. I do advise caution when you use them, but they are now so ingrained into our digital culture that it would be crazy to stay away entirely; besides, you can learn a lot through participation.

I have accounts at all of those and many other sites. I use several of them regularly, notably Twitter, but I make sure that what I say publicly on other sites is reflected on my own home base. This is usually possible, as I'll explain below, because Twitter and many other services give you a fairly easy way to push what you create using them out to other places.

There two basic ways to create your home base. The easy approach is to make a page, or collection of pages, using a free service. There are any number of sites that provide such services, including <u>Google Sites</u> and <u>Tumblr</u>. You might consider Blogger or WordPress.com, both of which offer profile pages among other parts of their free blogging services, enough for your needs.

Keep in mind, though, that such sites don't provide these services just to be helpful. Just as with Flickr and YouTube, you're putting your information into their databases, not yours. And you're using their names to help promote yours.

The more complex approach, which gives you greater flexibility, safety (in some ways) and authority, is to be your own publisher. I recommend it.

Whichever way you go, what you put on your personal site is the most important thing. Let's look at that first.

I'm a Brand?

Who we are, at least in a public sense, is the sum of what we do, what we say and what others say about us. You can't control what others say. However, you can absolutely control what you do and say.

Your presence can take many forms in a social-media world. It can be a Facebook page. It can be Flickr photos or YouTube video uploads. Or Twitter tweets. Or your own blog. Or several of these, and perhaps some of the many other options.

As we'll discuss in an upcoming chapter, you need to be—today, at least—somewhat careful of what you say and how you say it. But it's more important that what you say reflects who you actually are, assuming you're someone the rest of us should respect.

Your personal brand matters a great deal in an era of rapid economic changes, because you may move from job to job, perhaps even creating your own, and even within a single company your career will evolve. A personal brand does not mean notoriety, though some people have made careers of being publicly outrageous. It does mean establishing a reputation, because part of being valuable is being known as more than a reliable cog in a system.

Your Home Page: A Portal to You

Whichever way you've decided to create your home base, the most critical thing is to make it worthwhile. Easy to say, right? Actually, it's not so hard to do.

What should go into your own home base? Many things, but a few are key. I advise including an About page, a blog and links to everything else you're doing on the Web (or as many as you can link to). How the page looks matters, but the content is the most critical element. And, of course, you want to be found.

My home page has a "static" blog post at the top—a post that holds its position no matter what new blog postings I may write. There, I briefly introduce myself and what I do, and I point to other relevant pages on the site, including a more detailed About page as well as my speaking calendar, contact information and, of course, the Mediactive site. I specifically ask readers to think of the site as "a portal to (almost) everything I'm doing, online and offline."

My blogging at dangillmor.com consists mostly of personal material, with some political, tech-related and other items as well that don't fit neatly into my professional blogging.

Surrounding my personal blog are links to, or full posts from, many of the places where I post things elsewhere on the Net. They include Twitter tweets, product and business reviews I've posted at Amazon and Yelp, my Dopplr travel calendar, Flickr photos and more. And, of course, there's a link to the Amazon sales page for my last book. How can all this appear so neatly on my page? Because of RSS, which I described in Chapter 3; those sites let me create RSS feeds of the material I create on them, which I can then easily import into my site.

How often should you update your home base? That's entirely up to you. If you're doing great stuff on Twitter or other sites that pour information into your home base, you may not need to do constant updates on your blog, but if this is the single place where you blog the most, I recommend updating it at least twice a week. Those updates may take the form of text postings, embedded videos, podcasts or just about anything else. Some of the best blogs, moreover, have lots of short posts with many links; remember that linking is one of the basic values of the Web. Whatever you create, you want it first of all to be worth your effort; even if you have only a few readers or viewers, you are the person whose critiques matter most in the end.

None of what I've described is complicated, though I keep wishing for a service that would make it even easier to aggregate this "daily me" onto my page more easily. New services are springing up to help you do it on their sites—we'll list them on the Mediactive site—and you can get most of this done if you use iGoogle, MyYahoo, NetVibes and several other big-name services.

However you do this, you should remember that you're never finished. For better or worse, your home base will always be a work in progress, because you are a work in progress.

About You

Your About page is where you get to define who you are and what is at the core of your work and thoughts. If you are doing creative media, especially journalism, your About page should also be the place where you disclose anything that might be (or be perceived as) a conflict of interest, though of course you should also disclose that in any postings you make about relevant topics, as noted earlier.

If you have a resume or CV, link to it from the About page, both as a downloadable PDF file and a Web-readable HTML file. If you give talks, consider posting your speaking calendar (for privacy and security reasons, some people don't do this).

You should always include a way for others to contact you. You can create a Web form for them to fill out, or you can provide an embedded email address and phone number, or you can do all of these things. You should also have a Contact link on your home page, and ideally on all pages via a menu at the top.

I don't change my About page very often, and you probably won't, either. Minor tweaks, yes, but this isn't the place for discussing every quarter-turn of the screw in your career or other goings-on. Define yourself here in the broadest terms. Blog the smaller stuff.

Your Blog

I'm not a blogging determinist. That is, I don't see blogs as hammers and all problems as nails. But blogs are the best way, so far, to provide updates on what you're doing and why.

You may well have another, professional blog devoted to your vocation or work life. You may want to blog only in one place, mixing the professional and personal. These are individual decisions and depend on how you work and whether you want to mix the personal with everything else in a deep way.

It's even possible that you might want to create a purely personal blog somewhere other than your home-base site, if you're worried that people might misunderstand who you are based on its contents. If you feel the need for that kind of content segregation, consider whether to make that other blog pseudonymous (something I don't recommend but that is sometimes necessary).

What you blog on your home site is less relevant than the way you do it. If you post items full of misspellings and grammatical errors, people will notice. Taking care matters. If your posts are tedious and self-centered, people will notice that, too. Self-awareness also matters.

As noted earlier, your update frequency is up to you. The only rule that matters: Do what feels right to you.

When I comment at someone else's site, especially if I'm challenging what they've said about me or my work, I try to post an item about it on my own blog. This works both ways. I've been embroiled in a few major disputes over the years, and when that happens I make sure to talk about the issues on my own site, and to point back to my own thoughts from the comments elsewhere.

I strongly encourage opening your blog to comments. It's possible that no one will ever comment, but if you don't give people the opportunity to respond you are telling them you're not really interested in what they have to say. That defeats the conversational nature of media and can reflect poorly on you.

Most blogging software and services give you options for handling comments. I've set mine up so that I have to personally approve the first posting by anyone commenting for the first time; after that, they're free to post. I also use anti-spam add-ons to my blogs, because the spammers love to pollute blog comments the way they try to ruin everything else they touch.

Look and Feel

I'm a fan of simplicity. If I can't understand the purpose of a website at first glance, I'm not inclined to stick around, much less come back.

This is where blogs have a big advantage over other kinds of software. They're instantly recognizable for what they are, and modern blogging services offer a variety of ways to easily create sidebars and other ancillary material. The downside is that users tend to pick popular blog themes, which can make them feel less unique.

A new wrinkle in the look-and-feel category is the rise of mobile technology: More and more people are looking at the world through small devices with small screens. Be sure to check out the way your site looks on a mobile phone. If it's a gigantic mess, find a way to make it usable even on a small device. (See our online discussion of this at Mediactive.com.)

Whatever you decide about how your site looks, remember that in the end your taste is your own. Do it your way.

Being Found

If no one can find what you've said about yourself, you might as well not have said it. Which means that if search engines can't find you, you might as well not exist.

You should try to make your home-base site the first item on the first page of search results for your name, particularly in Google. This is not a matter of faking out the search companies—they look extremely askance at such attempts—but rather of providing them with the kind of information they need to recognize your page as the definitive item about you.

This may be difficult if you have an extremely common name or share the same (or even a similar) name with a celebrity. But if you're the John Smith who blogs about mobile phones and lives in Seattle, you should be able to be found by anyone who has the slightest idea of who they're looking for.

Commenting on other people's sites typically won't help get you into search rankings, though that shouldn't stop you from doing it. The blog comment spammers have so polluted the system that most blogging software now tells search engines not to look at the links in comments.

Because search is so important, the field of "search engine optimization" (SEO) has evolved into a huge and somewhat controversial business. At mediactive.com we'll be creating a list of some reputable SEO sites and companies, as well as offering some specific tips on how to optimize your home base so people can find you.

"YourSpace"—Owning Your Words

In the late 1980s I signed up for an account at an online bulletin-board system called The WELL, short for Whole Earth 'Lectronic Link. The WELL was way ahead of its time in almost every way, but one in particular stands out even now. Users were greeted with this language:

> *You own your own words.*

The context was primarily about responsibility, which we've discussed in earlier chapters and will return to in Chapter 9. But there was another context as well: literal ownership, that "no claims on your copyrights were being made by The WELL, and that you would be responsible for enforcing those rights."

There was a catch, though. Suppose the WELL went out of business. What would happened to my words? They'd disappear.

Fast forward to 2009, when Facebook launched a feature that became immediately popular: It gave users a way to have URLs—Web addresses—that included their actual real names or recognizable words chosen by the users. I signed up, and my Facebook home page became http://www.facebook.com/dangillmor instead of the previous URL, which looked something like "http://www.facebook.com/234030i8234x2f."

I did the same over at Google for my home page there. And I made sure that on the other social networks and services I used the most, I grabbed the dangillmor name, if possible; it's my username on Twitter and Skype, for example.

There are a huge number of services available today, and I have every incentive to try for the dangillmor name at as many as possible. One reason is to avoid confusion or semi-forgery. I'm not especially worried that someone will take over my identity in this way, but there's no reason to invite trouble. Moreover, new services have emerged that will help you—for a sometimes-substantial fee—nail down the username of your choice, assuming it isn't already taken, at dozens or even hundreds of sites.

But nailing down my own name raised a bigger question: Did I—do I—actually own my own name at on those services? The answer is an emphatic "No," because in reality I don't own the information I put into other people's sites and services—and that information specifically includes the vanity URL I'm permitted to claim.

This should be clear enough. But when Facebook expunged one of its users in 2008, the event set off a mini-firestorm among people who care about such things, prompting Daniel Solove to post this admonishment at the Concurring Opinions blog:

> (Y)ou exist on Facebook at the whim of Facebook. The Facebook dieties [sic] can zap your existence for reasons even more frivolous than those of the Greek gods. Facebook can banish you because you're wearing a blue T-shirt in your photo, or because it selected you at random, or because you named your blog Above the Law rather than Below the Law.

> On the one hand, this rule seems uncontroversial. After all, it is Facebook's website. They own their site, and they have the right to say who gets to use it and who doesn't.

> But on the other hand, people put a lot of labor and work into their profiles on the site. It takes time and effort to build a network of friends, to upload data, to write and create one's

profile. Locking people out of this seizes all their work from them. It's like your employer locking you out of your office and not letting you take your things. Perhaps at the very least banished people should be able to reclaim the content of their profiles. But what about all their "friends" on the network? People spend a lot of time building connections, and they can't readily transplant their entire network of friends elsewhere.

Since this incident, Facebook has opened up the user information in several ways, including letting users access their basic feeds from other websites and desktop applications, but only in specific ways that adhere to Facebook's strict rules. Facebook still controls the information, though it graciously (ahem) allows you to download what you've created there. So the reality is still this: It is Facebook's site, and they have every right to enforce their own rules, whether wise or ridiculous. Due process? It's not a judicial system, and we shouldn't treat or even imagine it that way.

The real issue is why users put so much of their own lives up on the site. Most, I suspect, have no idea that what they post is only partly their own, if at all. As with so many other services people use on today's Web, they may find out the hard way down the road. It's the risk we take when we make ourselves subject to the whims of little gods.

Mastering Your Domain

To the extent that such things are ownable, I own the Internet domain dangillmor.com. (I also own gillmor.com and a bunch of other domains including Mediactive.com, the website that hosts this project.)

What's a domain? It's your address on the Internet. Actually, it's a translation from a series of numbers—dangillmor.com is actually 207.58.180.217—that computers recognize via a series of cooperative agreements that have been established over the years. Without the Domain Name System, or DNS, the Net wouldn't work.

You don't need to care much about that. All you need to do is find a registrar: a company that registers your preferred domain name for an annual fee. Registrars abound, including big companies like Yahoo! that offer registration as one of many products, big registrars like Network Solutions and smaller firms like Tucows' Hover.com service. As with all kinds of businesses, cheap is not always synonymous with good. Several registrars have gone out of business in recent years, causing major headaches for their customers. Wikipedia offers a list of widely used registrars.

What's the best domain name? Your own name, for most people. If you can get the domain that goes FirstnameLastname.com, you should. If you have an uncommonly spelled name, there's a very good chance you can get it. If it's a common name, that's harder, but you can try for a *.net* or *.org* domain, or one of many others in the marketplace.

But you may want an entirely different kind of domain name, one that reflects a particular interest. How can you find a good one? Contrary to popular belief, all the good domains are not already taken. True, I got gillmor.com back in the early days of the Web (and stupidly didn't nail down others that turned out to be valuable, because I lacked the imagination to realize what a marketplace domain names would become). But in 2008, when I was looking for a good domain name for the Knight Center for Digital Media Entrepreneurship at Arizona State University, the name startupmedia.org was available.

I'm agnostic about whether you need to be a dot-com—that is, have an address that ends with ".com"—or whether it's just as good to use *.org* (typically for non-profits), *.net* or another so-called "top-level" domain. There are all kinds of these available now, including *.me*, aimed at personal sites. For now I'd suggest sticking with the major ones. (I'd avoid .info, which seems to be a spammer favorite.)

If you have an idea for a domain, the easiest way to see if it's already taken is to visit the registrar and attempt to obtain it. You'll know immediately if someone else has it. Some registrars offer suggestions, including related names. But my favorite way to come up with a domain name is to use one of the clever Web services that let you play with words and names, mixing and matching until you've discovered something that works. One of my favorites is NameStation.com, which lets you play with a variety of combinations until you find something you like, and also checks its availability.

Hosting

Once you have a domain, you have to decide where to host it. This means finding a service that provides servers and bandwidth. Many registrars do both, and this is certainly the simplest way to go. There are hundreds of hosting companies to choose from; the key is to find one that meets your needs and offers the best combination of price, reliability and service. As with registrars, your options range from companies like

Yahoo! to boutique services like the one I use, where, again, I know and trust the owner.

A good hosting company will give you easy ways to create your site on its servers. My hosting company, for example, will set up a WordPress blog for me, and gives me online tools that let me create sites using Drupal and many other, more flexible content-management systems (CMSs). You'll also get email services when you sign up with one of these companies. This has its own value. Rather than using the email from the Internet Service Provider where I live, I get my mail at dangillmor.com— a domain that stays with me even if I move and change ISPs. Of course, services like Gmail and Yahoo! mail also offer this portability, but I'd rather keep my mail archives (the messages I choose to save, far from all of them) on my computers than on someone else's.

Hosting may sound like a pain. And to some degree it can be. You may not need to get complicated in any way, though, if you just want to create a simple home base using platform-specific software.

For example, you could start a blog at WordPress.com, which offers hosted blogging services and gives you excellent flexibility in terms of the look and feel, though you can customize even more if you have your own WordPress (or other CMS) installation. Then, when you've created your blog, you can point it—for a fee—to your personal domain. Outsiders who go to your domain address will see the blog, which is hosted by WordPress, but they'll see it as part of your own domain. If you do this, be sure to get a backup drive that backs up all of your data on a regular basis.

Information Safety

I just emailed this chapter to myself.

Call me paranoid or merely careful, but I've become an advocate of relentless, systematic backups of data. And when I post on other peoples sites, I look for ways to take out what I've put in.

Backing Up

If you don't back up your data, you are a fool. Sorry to be so blunt, but I don't offer this as nice-to-do advice.

My practice is fairly simple. I "clone" the hard drive of my computer—i.e., make an exact copy—once a week. Every day, I back up my current work files. I email my chapter drafts to myself. And I'm looking into the online backup services—saving work into what people call "the cloud"—that are gaining popularity among the techno-cogniscenti.

Even with this regime, I still end up losing things, most typically when a word-processing program—yes, Microsoft, I'm talking about you—crashes in the middle of a chapter and somehow the changes I thought I'd saved go missing. This doesn't happen very often, but it's annoying and part of the process.

One way to have this happen less is to compose more of your drafts online, via services like Google Documents. The risk of putting everything into the cloud is that sometimes even companies you expect to be reliable lose things. (A Microsoft-owned mobile data service, appropriately called Danger, had just such an issue in mid-2009.) We did some of the editing of this book in Google Documents with no mishap, but I was careful to download the Mediactive Book folder frequently, just in case.

Your blog and other home-base material is almost certainly living in the cloud. You should check with your hosting provider to ensure that it's performing regular backups. WordPress, Drupal and other packages offer options to make backups of the data, on the server or downloadable to your own computer.

My former employer deleted my entire archive of blog postings—not just once, but twice.

The first time, around 2001, was because of a platform change combined with the company's misguided understanding of what the Web was about; removing history struck me as perverse and still does. The second time was after I left Knight Ridder in 2005; the reason given was that it would be too costly to keep running the server—something that again struck me as bizarre. But they had the right to delete it, even if I though they were doing a dramatically wrong thing.

In 2009, we got a lot of it back, and we have restored most of the old Knight Ridder blog to a site at Bayosphere.com (that's another story, which I won't tell here, but you can read it at the site).

What prompted the project was the Web-sleuthing of blog historian Rudolf Ammann, who used the wonderful Internet Archive to locate many of the earliest posts. This made me wonder if it might be possible to resurrect a lot more or even most of what had gone missing.

Pete Kaminski, a friend and technical whiz, took on the task. He's done an incredible job of spidering, scraping, parsing and otherwise pulling as much as possibleout of the Archive.

We're not nearly done. We're looking for more of the EJournal, of course—dozens or perhaps hundreds of posts are still missing, and may be gone for good.

I learned a big lesson from this experience. I no longer rely entirely on the good graces of other people, including employers, to preserve what I've created, much less keep it available for you to see. I try to rely on myself.

Portable Data

When you start a blog at WordPress.com, you'll discover something wonderful, should you dig deep enough into the system settings: You can take it with you if you decide to leave. WordPress offers a backup system that includes a way to email the entire database of content to yourself at regular intervals, and the open-source WordPress community has written many plug-ins to make this and similar processes easy and robust.

Even when you can readily get your data out of a site or service, that doesn't mean you're home free. Downloading the WordPress database is only the first step if you want to move it into another blogging software system. It can be done, but it's not always easy.

The WordPress community is serious about this issue, though, and it's offering support to a movement that is gaining strength in this era of multiple sites and services where we post words, pictures, videos and more. The movement wants to make our data portable, so that we aren't locked into someone else's system or method of doing things.

In general, when you're using other people's services you should always look for evidence that you can get out what you've put in. You should also keep copies of pictures and videos you upload.

Owning Your Honor

We have no idea yet what it means for mostly private citizens to live semi-public lives in the Digital Age. We'll be figuring this out for years, even decades, to come.

But we do know that we have to define ourselves, or risk having others define us. They'll do so in any event, but if we don't make our own case for who we are, we're missing an opportunity.

Chapter 8

Entrepreneurs Will Save Journalism, and You Could Be One of Them

Did the title of this chapter scare you? It shouldn't—but I'm going to ask you to stretch your mind just a bit in the pages ahead.

In this chapter I want to discuss, celebrate and speculate about how journalism is moving into the new era. We are racing ahead because so many people are trying new ideas and creating startup enterprises around them.

Maybe you'll be one of them, at whatever level you may choose to venture into the arena—a blog on a topic where you can be the among the best guides, a community mail list, a video service, or anything that you are passionate about. You may want to make some money at it, or you may be motivated solely to help your community. Remember, the barrier to entry is close to zero, and you don't need anyone's permission.

Even if you aren't planning to do any of those things, you'll find what follows useful for this reason: Entrepreneurship is journalism's future—the future of pretty much all enterprises, for that matter—so we all need to appreciate how it works, and how it is working.

As you read this, please remember to keep the core mediactive principles in mind. If we are not honorable in our practices, all of our innovation will fall short.

A Prescient Warning, and Unheeded Advice

Some of the most successful entrepreneurs of recent decades have come from the technology arena. One of the most brilliant business leaders in modern history is <u>Andy Grove</u>, a co-founder of Silicon Valley giant <u>Intel Corp.</u>, where he served as chief executive and chairman. In the 1980s he led the company through a wrenching transition, when he and his colleagues changed Intel's focus from computer memory, a business they were losing to Asian competitors, to the central processor chips that became the heart of the world's personal computers. With that move, the genius of which became clear only much later, Grove gave Intel its future—at least for the next several decades—and assured his own place as one of America's great business leaders.

Grove, who is also an author and teacher, believes deeply in journalism's importance, and he is never shy about speaking his mind. Never was that more clear than in April 1999, when he took the stage at the annual meeting of the <u>American Society of Newspaper Editors</u>, held that year in San Francisco. In a conversation with <u>Jerry Ceppos</u>, former editor of Silicon Valley's once-great daily newspaper, the <u>*San Jose Mercury News*</u>, Grove warned the editors that their time was running short: Newspapers faced a financial meltdown. He wasn't the first to issue such a warning, and hardly the last. But the degree to which he was ignored remains instructive, and sad.

At the <u>ASNE conference</u>, he passed this same message on to the editors themselves:

> You're where Intel was three years before the roof fell in on us. You're heading toward a strategic inflection point, and three years from now, maybe, it's going to be obvious.... And my history of the technology industry is you cannot save yourself out of a strategic inflection point. You can save yourself deeper into the morass that you're heading to, but you can only invest your way out of it, and I really wonder how many people who are in charge of the business processes of journalism understand that.

Grove was right about the trajectory, though a bit premature about the timing. He was even more right about the industry's likely response: rampant cost-cutting, much too little investment and, above all, the failure to appreciate the value of entrepreneurial thinking.

How times have changed. The entrepreneurial, startup culture has infiltrated journalism in a big way—because so many people are trying new things, mostly outside of big enterprises but also inside the more progressive ones; because Digital Age experimentation is so inexpensive; and because we can already see the outlines of what's emerging.

Although the transition will be messy, we're heading toward a great new era in media and journalism. To be sure, we are losing some things we need, at least temporarily. But I'm an optimist, because if we do the transition right we'll have a more diverse and vibrant media ecosystem. And by "we" I mean you, me and everybody.

"Ecosystem" and "diversity" are key words here. The dangers of monocultures—systems that have little or no diversity—are well understood, even though they still exist in many areas, such as modern farming and finance. Because monocultures are inherently unstable, the results are catastrophic when they fail—as we saw with Wall Street in 2008. A diverse ecosystem, by contrast, isn't as threatened by failures, because they tend to be smaller and are replaced by new successes. In a diverse and vibrant capitalist economy, the failure of enterprises is tragic only for the specific constituencies of those enterprises, but what the Austrian economist Joseph Schumpeter called "creative destruction," assuming that we have fair and enforceable rules of the road for all, ensures the long-term sustainability of the economy.

Recall from Chapter 1 that the journalistic ecosystem of the past half-century was dominated by a small number of giant companies. Those enterprises, aided by governmental policies and manufacturing-era efficiencies of scale, controlled the marketplace and grew bigger and bigger. The collision of Internet-fueled technology and traditional media's business model, which is heavily reliant on advertising sales, was cataclysmic for the big companies.

But is it catastrophic for the communities and societies the big companies served? In the short term, it's plainly problematic, at least when we consider Big Journalism's role as a watchdog (inconsistent though the dominant companies have been in serving that role). But the worriers appear to assume that we can't replace what we will lose. They have no faith in the restorative power of a diverse, market-based ecosystem, because they have little or no experience of being part of one.

The diversity that's coming—in fact, is already arriving—is breathtaking. As we all come to demand better from our information sources, and create trustworthy information ourselves, we'll have the choices we need at our fingertips.

And remember this: The largest companies in the world started with individual people's ideas. Maybe yours will someday be one of them. Even if you don't really believe that, don't ever assume you can't try. Here's why.

Experimentation Is Cheap

In digital media, the cost of trying new ideas is heading toward zero. That means lots and lots of people will be—and already are—testing the possibilities.

Clay Shirky has done some acute analysis of this phenomenon. He points to the lesson of Sourceforge, the site where open-source software developers post projects for other people to download, analyze and hopefully improve, and for non-technical people to download and use.

Clay notes that the overwhelming majority of Sourceforge projects are, by any definition, failures. Among the more than 150,000 projects that run on the Windows operating system, the most successful have tens to hundreds of millions of downloads. But if you go down the list, many even in the top 25 percent have fewer than 1,000 downloads—which in a practical sense is essentially none at all. (In more than a third of all projects, no one has cared enough even to look, much less help out or download the software.) But those tens of thousands of failures are individually inexpensive, and they set a stage for the few but vitally important successes. What does this imply? As Clay wrote in the _Harvard Business Review_ in 2007:

> [T]he low cost of failure means that someone with a new idea doesn't have to convince anyone else to let them try it—there are few institutional barriers between thought and action.

Similarly, the R&D that the news industry should have done years ago is now being done in a highly distributed way. Yes, some is being done by people inside media companies, but most is not—and increasingly it won't be. It'll take place in universities, in corporate labs, in garages and at kitchen tables. (I wish there was a more organized way to find and share what's happening, and in Chapter 11 I describe a think-tank approach to doing just that.)

In other words, not only don't you need permission to create media, but you don't need much money, either. This is one reason I'm so optimistic about the future of media, and of journalism.

Experiments by Traditional Media

Although I'm less optimistic about traditional news organizations' willingness or ability to change, I definitely don't want to write them off entirely. Not only are they needed, when they do their job well, but most are still making operating profits. Moreover, the traditional media have only just begun to experiment themselves. And the ones that are experimenting are doing wondrous things; we talk about many of them on Mediactive.com. The industry experiments have mostly tended to be on the journalistic side, however. The business innovation? Not so much. Even here, though, there are glimmers of ideas, mostly due to the sheer panic in executive suites.

At the end of 2009, for example, media company executives were falling all over themselves to assert their determination to start charging for what they were allegedly giving away. (Never mind that they'd been essentially giving it away for decades, as noted in Chapter 1.) My reaction: Heck yes, give it a try. As I write this, the New York Times appears to be on the verge of putting up a "pay wall," as people call this kind of venture.

I doubt pay walls will work, in most cases. There's too much content available for no charge, and too little added value evident in what the news organizations say they want audiences to pay for. But there's plenty of evidence that people will pay for specialized content that they believe they need. I subscribe to the online editions of the *Wall Street Journal* and *Consumer Reports*, for example, and as long as their subscription rates are modest I'll keep doing so. Magazines and some newspapers are working on a format and billing system, possibly tied to tablet devices. I wish them well.

In early 2009, I tried stirring the pot a bit, with a suggestion that a few top news organizations could charge for what they produce if they merged outright. In a post on the blog BoingBoing, I asked:

> What would happen if some top English language journalism organizations simply merged and started charging for their breaking news and commentary about policy, economics and other national/international topics? That is, what if they were to combine for critical mass and keep most of their journalism off the public Internet for a few days after publication but then make the archives freely available?

My list of top organizations included the *New York Times*, the *Wall Street Journal*, the *Washington Post*, the *Financial Times*, *The Economist*, *Atlantic Monthly*, *Washington Monthly*, and *The New Yorker*.

"I don't know the combined annual newsroom cost of these organizations, but I'd be surprised if it was even $750 million," I said. "Let's go wild and call it $1 billion, so we can pay for lawyers, Web developers, accountants, and a bunch of other folks who'd need to be part of the operation." The merged enterprise could generate much more than that with 2 million subscribers paying a modest $10 a week rate.

Naturally, I got lots of pushback on this idea. But I do know this: I'd pay, gladly, for such a product.

Government Intervention

Some big news organizations and their corporate parents have latched, sadly, onto a much more alarming, anti-capitalistic notion:

government (read: taxpayer) help. They've <u>talked about</u> changing copyright laws to prevent what they call "free-riding"—the notion that online media aggregators are taking the value from their use of the information from other sources without giving anything in return. They've talked about direct subsidies, and more.

There's a long history of government assistance, including but not limited to licenses to use the airwaves for broadcasters as well as postal subsidies for mailing newspapers and magazines. Most of what's being proposed today, however, is ill-advised or even counterproductive. We need to let the marketplace work before concluding that taxpayer intervention is in any way necessary.

This isn't to say that politicians and bureaucrats couldn't improve key laws and regulations that have an impact on media. In copyright and a number of other areas—notably broadband policy—we can do much better. I'll discuss this in Chapter 11.

The "Startup Culture"

What is entrepreneurship all about? Whether you're doing it inside or outside of another enterprise, here are some key features (credit for much of this goes to my colleague, <u>CJ Cornell</u>):

- **Ownership**: This doesn't necessarily mean owning stock in a company, though of course there's nothing wrong with that. As CJ explains to our students, it's about owning the process, and the outcome, of what you're doing.

- **Focus**: If you can't focus, you can't succeed in a startup. I know this from experience; my Bayosphere project failed in part because I believed—contrary to wise admonitions from one of my investors—that I could do lots of things at once.

- **Ambiguity**: Startups are full of ambiguities and even chaos. If you're the kind of person who can't deal with this, you may be ill-suited for entrepreneurship. Understand a rule of startups: Your ultimate product is likely to be vastly different than what you originally imagined, and it'll keep evolving.

- **Resourcefulness**: Startups have to use what's available. If you have everything on your wish list, you're either over-funded or under-creative.

- **Speed**: Entrepreneurs move fast. They change with evolving conditions and take advantage of opportunities that emerge and disappear in short order. They make decisions and move forward.

- **Innovation**: You can innovate by being more efficient or thorough, not just by inventing new technologies. The Googles are few and far between, but innovators often connect dots where others can't imagine the connections.

- **Risk**: Appreciating risk is essential to the entrepreneurial process, but it doesn't belong at the top of the list. You minimize the risk when you can, understanding that you can't eliminate it.

The process of entrepreneurship differs from project to project. In the digital media space, however, I'd suggest the following:

1. Start with good idea, and above all follow your personal passion. An entrepreneur who doesn't believe in her goal with every fiber of her being has already started to fail, in the words of <u>Dave Winer</u>, a serial entrepreneur and pioneer in digital media.

2. Develop it quickly and collaboratively, using off-the-shelf tools when possible and writing code only to create the parts you can't find elsewhere. Be open with others about what you are doing. "Stealth mode" projects can and do work out, but most ideas will find more traction with the help of others who care about what you're doing.

3. Launch *before* you think you're fully ready, because when you launch you're just getting started. Who says? My friend <u>Reid Hoffman,</u> founder of the <u>LinkedIn</u> network and a prescient investor in Internet companies, once told me with reference to the launch of a consumer Internet company, "If you aren't completely embarrassed by your website when you launch, you waited too long."

4. Following on the previous point, assume you'll be in beta mode for some time. You will have bugs and problems. Fix what's broken and keep iterating.

5. If you see that the project is going to fail, don't prolong it. Don't waste time, and don't spend investors' money after it's clear you should stop. This may sound like a contradiction of the first point, and in some ways it is; remember what I said about ambiguity?

6.   Repeat. A smart failure teaches valuable lessons. Internal entrepreneurship in companies, also called "intrapreneurship," should be especially forgiving of failure, assuming it's not stupid or reckless.

While large enterprises can innovate, in the digital media world they may be better off buying or licensing from startups. Bill Joy, co-founder of Sun Microsystems, put it best when he said, "No matter who you are, most of the smartest people work for someone else."

A good idea is only the beginning of a great startup. Entrepreneurs *must* appreciate the hard realities of running a business. This is as true for a non-profit as for a for-profit enterprise; making them sustainable is a core mission.

I hear about dozens of startups every month. Most will fail, but I have to stress again: This is not a flaw in the system. It's a feature.

If I Ran a News Organization, Part 1

Traditional news organizations have long had a low entrepreneurial quotient, for a wide variety of reasons. Near the top of the list is that their journalists have been walled off from business operations.

Management requires them to keep away from the advertising department, as if they'd get a terminal disease if they had much contact. This separation of church and state, as we journalists called it with such hubris, came from good motives: to make sure the advertisers—the main customers of the newspaper, if the people who supply the most revenues are the main customers—don't dictate or even influence news coverage. This separation was always something of a fiction, given publishers' and broadcasting station managers' business duties and influence over the people who worked for them, but it did serve a purpose.

My experiences on the business side of life—both early in my adulthood, when I ran a musical enterprise, and more recently as co-founder of a failed startup, as an investor, and as co-founder of a successful startup—have persuaded me that the so-called church-state wall has been one of 20th-century pro journalism's cardinal flaws. By all means, tell advertisers that they don't run the news operations (and mean it). But a journalist who has no idea how his industry really works from a business perspective is missing way too much of the big picture.

If I ran a news organization today, whether a startup or part of an established company, I'd want to be sure that the journalists understood, appreciated and embraced the new arena we all inhabit. That emphatically includes how business works. I'd want them to understand the variety of financial models that support media—especially the organization that employed them—and to be versed in the lingo of <u>CPM</u> (cost of advertising per thousand impressions), <u>SEO</u> (search engine optimization) and the like. I would not ask journalists to grub for the most page views, a new trend that tends to bring out the worst in media, but would very much want them to know what was happening in all parts of their enterprise, not just the content area. Maybe—just maybe—if the journalists really understood their business, one of them would have one of the golden ideas it needs to prosper instead of crumble.

There aren't all that many ways to make media enterprises sustainable. Among them are subscriptions, advertising, donations, memberships, voluntarism and ancillary services that cross-subsidize the journalism. Two examples: A law professor might run a legal blog that's subsidized by her employer (and thus carries no advertising) and which advances her career. Or a journalistic enterprise might hold money-making conferences.

I'm intrigued by any number of new ideas I've seen from the business side of media lately, and I spend a fair amount of time in the Mediactive blog pointing them out. For the people doing these experiments, the ethical issues are more real than ever. The closer the journalists get to the people paying for the journalism, the more issues they face about holding fast to those basic principles. Transparency becomes more central than ever.

If I Ran a News Organization, Part 2

Call me old-fashioned, but I still believe it's possible to have a news organization that combines 21st-century tools and tactics with the timeless principles of excellence and honor. We are nearly free from the printing presses, the expensive broadcasting gear and especially the top-down approach of the past. Tomorrow's great journalism practitioners and organizations will believe in—and work in—a culture that embraces the possibilities of this emergent conversational and collaborative space.

Although what follows are editorial suggestions, not business ones—I recognize that none of these ideas matters if the business fails—they are essential to my ideal enterprise. Besides, most of these could be implemented with no additional cost, and I'm absolutely convinced that they'd help create news product that's worthy of audience support. A business that doesn't respect and value its customers has no future.

So, here are some of the things I'd insist on if I ran a news organization.

First, we would invite our audience to participate in the journalism process in a broad variety of ways, including through crowdsourcing, audience blogging, wikis and many other means. We'd make it clear that we're not looking for free labor—and work to create a system that rewards contributors beyond a mere pat on the back—and that we want above all to promote a multi-directional flow of news and information in which the audience plays a vital role.

To that end, transparency would be a core element of our journalism. One example of many: Every print article would have an accompanying box called "Things We Don't Know"—a list of questions our journalists couldn't answer in their reporting. TV and radio stories would mention the key unknowns. Whatever the medium, the organization's website would include an invitation to the audience to help fill in the holes—and every story has holes.

We would embrace the hyperlink in every possible way. Our website would include the most comprehensive possible listing of other media in our community, whether we were a community of geography or interest. We'd link to all relevant blogs, photo streams, video channels, database services and other material we could find, and use our editorial judgment to highlight the ones we considered best for the members of the community. And we'd liberally link from our journalism to other work and source material relevant to the topic under discussion, recognizing that we are not oracles but guides.

We would create a service to notify online readers, should they choose to sign up for it, of errors we learned about in our journalism. Users of this service could choose to be notified of major errors only (in our judgment) or all errors, however insignificant we might believe them to be.

We'd make conversation an essential element of our mission. Among other things:

- If we were a local newspaper, the editorial and op-ed pages would publish the best of, and be a guide to, the conversation the community was having with itself online and in other public forums, whether hosted by the news organization or someone else. Our website would link to a variety of commentary from the usual suspects, but syndicated columns would almost never appear in the print edition.

- Editorials would appear in blog format, as would letters to the editor.

- We would encourage comments and forums, but in moderated spaces that both encouraged the use of real names and insisted on (and enforced) civility.

- Comments from people using verified real names would be listed first (i.e., given priority on the page).

We'd routinely point to our competitors' work, including (and maybe especially) the best of the new entrants, e.g., bloggers who cover specific niches. When we'd covered the same topic, we'd link to other people's work to enable our audience to gain more perspectives. We'd also talk about and point to competitors when they covered things we'd missed or ignored.

Beyond routinely pointing to competitors, we would make a special effort to cover and follow up on their most important work, in contrast to the common practice today of pretending it didn't exist. As a basic rule, the more we wished we'd done the journalism ourselves, the more prominent would be the exposure we'd give the other folks' work. This would have at least two beneficial effects. First, we'd help persuade our community of an issue's importance. Second, we'd help people understand the value of solid journalism, no matter who does it.

The more we believed an issue was of importance to our community, the more relentlessly we'd stay on top of it ourselves. If we concluded that continuing down a current policy path was a danger, we'd actively campaign to persuade people to change course. This would have meant, for example, loud and persistent warnings about the danger of the blatantly obvious housing/financial bubble that inflated during the past decade.

We would refuse to do stenography and call it journalism. If one faction or party to a dispute were lying, we would say so, and provide the accompanying evidence. If we learned that a significant number of people in our community believed a lie about an important person or issue, we would make it part of our ongoing mission to help them understand the truth.

We would replace certain Orwellian and PR-speakish words and common expressions with more neutral, precise language. If someone we interviewed misused language, we would paraphrase instead of running direct quotes. Examples of phrasing we'd change include:

- We would not write that someone "is worth" some amount of money. We'd say he or she has financial holdings of that amount, or that his or her wealth is such and such.

- We wouldn't say that health care paid for by taxpayers is free.

- The activity that takes place in casinos is gambling, not gaming.

- There are no death taxes. There can be inheritance or estate taxes.

- Certain violent practices for which America and its allies have successfully prosecuted others on war-crimes charges are torture, not "enhanced interrogation techniques."

- Piracy is what people carrying guns on the high seas do: capturing ships, stealing cargo and turning crews and passengers into hostages, or sometimes murdering them. Piracy does not describe what people do when they post digital music on file-sharing networks.

We'd assess risks honestly. Journalists constantly use anecdotal evidence in ways that frighten the public into believing a problem is larger than it actually is. We would make it a habit a) not to extrapolate a wider threat from weird or tragic anecdotes, b) to regularly discuss the major risks we face and contrast them statistically with the minor ones, and c) to debunk the most egregious examples of horrible stories that spark unnecessary fear or even panic.

Our archives would be freely available, with permalinks—Web addresses that don't change or disappear — on every single thing we'd published as far back as possible, and we would provide easy digital access to help other people use our journalism in ways we hadn't considered ourselves.

A core mission of our work would be to help people in the community become informed users of media, not passive consumers—and to understand not just how they can do this, but why they should. We would work with schools and other institutions that recognize the necessity of critical thinking. (See Chapter 10.)

We would not run anniversary stories and commentary except in the rarest of circumstances. They are a refuge for lazy and unimaginative journalists.

We would never publish lists of 10. They're a prop as well.

Except in the most dire of circumstances—such as a threat to a whistle-blower's life, liberty or livelihood—we would not quote or paraphrase unnamed sources in any of our journalism. If we did, we would need persuasive evidence from the source as to why we should break this rule, and we'd explain why we had done it in our coverage. Moreover, when we did grant anonymity, we'd offer our audience the following guidance: We believe this is one of the rare times when anonymity is justified, but we urge you to exercise appropriate skepticism.

If we granted anonymity and learned that the source had lied to us, we would consider the confidentiality agreement to have been breached by that person and would expose his or her duplicity and identity. Sources would know of this policy before we published. We'd further look for examples where our competitors had been tricked by sources they didn't name, and then do our best to expose them, too.

The word "must"—as in "the president must do this or that"— would be banned from editorials or other commentary from our own journalists, and we'd strongly discourage it from contributors. It is a hollow word and only emphasizes powerlessness. If we wanted someone to do something, we'd try persuasion instead, explaining why it's a good idea (though almost certainly not one that originated with us) and what the consequences will be if the advice is ignored.

For any person or topic we covered regularly, we would provide a "baseline"—an article (or video, etc.) where people could start if they were new to the topic—and point prominently to that "start here" piece from any new coverage. We might use a modified Wikipedia approach to keep the article current with the most important updates. The point would be to offer context, giving unprepared readers a way to get up to speed quickly and others a way to recall the context of the issue.

For any coverage where this made sense, we'd tell our audience members how they could act on the information we'd just given them. This would typically take the form of a "What You Can Do" box or pointer.

We'd work in every possible way to help our audience know who's behind the words and actions we reported. People and institutions frequently try to influence the rest of us in ways that hide their participation in the debate, and we'd do our best to reveal who's spending the money and pulling the strings. When our competitors declined to reveal such things, or failed to ask obvious questions of their sources, we'd talk about their journalistic failures in our own coverage of the issues.

We'd publish no op-eds bylined by major politicians, executives or celebrities. These big names almost never actually write what appears under their bylines, and we're being just as dishonest as they are by publishing it. If they want to pitch a policy or cause, they should post it on their own web pages, and we'll be happy to point to those pages.

I could offer dozens more suggestions, but the ones I've listed strike me as key. More than a recipe, they add up to a sense of duty to the communities we serve. Even for organizations bound up in a legacy of "the way we've always done things," it's not too late to try something with the potential to turn a trend around.

Repeat After Me: Journalism's Future Is Bright

As I said back in the first chapter, I'm jealous of my students. I wish I could be their age, starting out when the slate is so blank, when the possibilities are so wide open. They, not my generation, will be among the entrepreneurs who invent the news organizations of the future that will welcome us as co-creators of journalism.

The kind of media environment we need, and, ultimately, the kind a democratic society needs to make informed decisions, won't come easily. The decisions that will make the new journalism possible lie not only with those who try to practice it, or even with their audience—the new era will require changes to the legal, social and economic environment. We'll look some of them in the following chapters.

Part III: Introduction

We're going to switch gears a bit here. Until now we've been focusing on our participation in media, as consumers and as creators. The next several chapters look more widely at topics that are not as much about what we can do individually as what we need to consider as a society.

Why the broader brush? Because the issues I'm going to discuss are intertwined with media, participatory media in particular. The success of mediactivity depends on them.

When we look at things like copyright and other legal issues, as we will do in the next chapter, we are looking directly at how well any of us may be able to participate in tomorrow's media. When we consider the social customs of the recent past, and agree that we need to update them in the new century's flourishing digital age, we are understanding another key part of our participatory culture.

And when we consider who should be bringing mediactive values to our children (and ourselves), we're considering a broader effect than the impact on our own immediate needs.

Our work won't be done even when we get all of this. I noted early in the book that we're only in the early days of this amazing and, I believe, wonderful evolution. That means we have a long way to go, and it's worth considering what pieces of the puzzle are still obviously missing. Of course, once we locate them, we'll realize how much more there is to do. We'll be working on this for our lifetimes. So will our grandchildren, for theirs.

As societies and within our narrower communities of geography and interest, we'll get closer and closer to something vital for the function of self-governing societies: a diverse, robust and trustworthy mediasphere. Remember, we can't do it alone.

Chapter 9

Laws and Norms

In the spring of 2008, the popular blog BoingBoing lampooned some terms of service that a company called MagicJack had imposed on users of its Internet telephone service, as well as a misleading visitor-counter on its website. Discussing the terms of service, BoingBoing's Rob Beschizza explained (among other things) that users had to agree that the company could analyze their calling patterns to send them targeted advertising, and that it could force customers to arbitrate any disputes in Florida.

MagicJack sued, claiming the posting had caused irreparable harm to its reputation. BoingBoing, an ad-supported business that's insured against defamation claims, was not intimidated and fought back. In 2010, a California court ruled that MagicJack had no case because what Beschizza had written was a reasonable portrayal of what MagicJack itself had published in its terms of service and on its website. The judge also ordered the company to pay a big portion of BoingBoing's legal fees.

Several of BoingBoing's contributors are friends of mine, and I was overjoyed to hear that they'd successfully fended off a company that was trying to use the courts to shut down protected free speech. The case highlighted the importance of a robust marketplace for ideas. But the bloggers' victory was also a reminder that some risks accompany the exercise of our First Amendment rights.

While the BoingBoing case was moving through the courts, America's media-critic-in-chief, President Barack Obama, cautioned a group of 14- and 15-year-olds to be careful about what they posted online. His advice was prompted, during a Virginia school visit, by a query from a student who'd announced his intention to become president some day. According to the White House's transcript, the current president offered, in the first of what he called "practical tips" for ambitious young people, this suggestion:

> I want everybody here to be careful about what you post on Facebook—because in the YouTube age, whatever you do, it will be pulled up again later somewhere in your life. And when

you're young, you make mistakes and you do some stupid stuff. And I've been hearing a lot about young people who, you know, they're posting stuff on Facebook, and then suddenly they go apply for a job and somebody has done a search and, so that's some practical political advice for you right there.

Obama's advice was conventional wisdom, and was undoubtedly correct in today's world. I hope he's wrong in tomorrow's.

The BoingBoing case and Obama's cautions, which I'll discuss in more detail later, combine all sorts of issues that we need to consider in a democratized media world: law, social customs and more. How we behave online has ramifications.

Let me reassure you: If you've taken to heart the principles I've outlined in earlier chapters, you can much more easily minimize whatever risks there may be in your own participation online. How? Be honorable. It's that simple.

That said, we can't reduce risk to zero, partly because the legal system invites abuses from people whose goal is to shut down speech they don't like. Meanwhile, the system is evolving to adapt to new challenges.

Laws increasingly determine how we can use online resources as active consumers. This starts with whether we can find the resources at all. Many governments take great pains to block what they see as dangerous (usually for them) or immoral material. According to the OpenNet Initiative, a project that documents Internet filtering and surveillance, a number of countries actively censor what their residents can readily see. Along with controlling what we get to see, both governments and private entities track our every move via digital surveillance.*

Some laws and regulations, especially in the copyright arena, give enormous power to large enterprises that make decisions about our Internet use. Others apply to everything from our comments on other people's sites to the material we publish on our own, as the BoingBoing example and others in this chapter will show.

---

*You might imagine this to be merely a Chinese problem, or an issue in Saudi Arabia and other places under authoritarian rule. Sadly, the U.S. government is making similar noises. As I write this, Congress is considering a bill, aimed at stopping copyright infringement, that would invite—and in some cases force—Internet service providers to block access to sites deemed to host troublesome material, even if those sites also host totally unobjectionable content.

Again, I don't want to scare you here. The odds that you will get in unjust legal trouble are slim. But as you'll see in the pages ahead, forewarned is forearmed; it's better to know about something ahead of time so you can prepare, however remote the possibility may be that you'll be affected.

Laws are only part of the issue, as Obama's cautions demonstrated. We also need to adjust some attitudes and learn some new skills— individually and as a society—in order to keep up with the collaborative communications tools that not only empower us in such amazing ways, but also can cause difficulties if we're not fully aware of what we're doing.

These attitudes and skills are about what sociologists call *norms*— principles of behavior that, according to Webster's definition, "guide, control, or regulate proper and acceptable behavior." When I use the word here, I'm talking about societal acceptance, about generally agreed ways to behave. In Japan, for example, it's a norm to take off your shoes when you enter someone's home, and bow when greeting someone; in America we tend to keep our shoes on and shake hands. I'm emphatically not talking about laws and regulations, which are enforced by governments; norms are enforced, if that's the right word, but by you and me.

The principles outlined in Chapters 2 and 5, which undergird this entire project, are fundamentally about norms, as is Obama's advice and some of the other material presented later in this chapter. There can be negative consequences for acting outside the norms, but you're generally free to do so as long as you don't mind the consequences.

Law and Order

Let's look at a few of the key legal issues first. These include the way laws affect our basic rights as users of media as well as our legal responsibilities in such areas as defamation, copyright and privacy.

Keep in mind that this survey is, once again, a high-altitude look down at the landscape, not a detailed map or a legal guide. I'm not a lawyer, and nothing here is intended to be legal advice.

Privacy and Surveillance

The same tools that give us such incredible freedom to create and share are also a cause for caution. As the Electronic Frontier Foundationsays, "New technologies are radically advancing our freedoms, but they are also enabling unparalleled invasions of privacy."

It's possible to invite some of the invasions, of course, even in routine use of the Web. If you sign up for mobile phone social networks that broadcast your location to friends and others who use the same services, you're giving up some privacy. If you post on Facebook, you're being public. As we'll discuss later in this chapter, we all need to think about how other people—including people we don't imagine to be following us—could make use of the information we radiate.

Beyond the information we release willingly is a cornucopia of information released about us by others. A GPS-enabled mobile phone tells the mobile network company and anyone with access to the carrier's data where you are and where you've been. And when you shop online, or even just browse, you are providing data that's the rough equivalent of having someone follow you around a shopping mall with a video camera, recording and storing everything you buy or even look at.

Americans know (because journalists have ferreted out the story) that their government created a vast and illegal surveillance system that was used to monitor American communications for years during the Bush administration. For all we know, that monitoring is still happening; the Obama government claims essentially all of the same rights as its predecessor to do what it pleases, never mind the Constitution.

That's bad enough, but the companies that provide digital technology and network services have unparalleled abilities to watch your every move as well. And many cyber-criminals floating around those networks (working remotely from places like Russia, in many cases) have the technical sophistication to play malevolent games with your communications, including financial ones.

There are laws supposedly protecting privacy, or at least misuse of data. The problem is that they're rarely enforced, and the penalties for violating them are not much of a deterrent.

Just as you need to put much sturdier locks on your door in a bad neighborhood, you need to take steps to preserve (what's left of) your privacy online. One of the most important measures is actually the simplest: Keep your software up to date, applying the bug fixes and security "patches" companies provide. Another is to use Web browser plug-ins such as the NoScript add-on for the Mozilla Firefox browser, which lets you block many of the kinds of drive-by attacks you can encounter in your routine Web browsing.

As you increase your mediactivity from the routine, it's honorable to give users of your blog or website as much privacy as possible, including protecting their data from being extracted and used by a hacker. Just as you need to keep the software you run on your own computer current, you should be as certain as you can be that your Web-hosting provider is doing the same on its own systems.

Sidebar: Privacy and Facebook—Why I Quit and Rejoined

I use Facebook for several reasons. One is my professional interest in keeping track of what's happening in the planet's largest social network, including what application developers and users are doing there. More personal is that some of my friends—actual friends—use the site, and Facebook helps me stay in touch with them.

But when Facebook made a dramatic change to its privacy structure at the end of 2009, I concluded I could no longer trust the service, even with the limited amount of things I've said and done there since I got an account several years ago. I continue to admire the company's accomplishments in many other ways, so why did I no longer feel safe and sound in the hands of Facebook?

Even though some of the changes made in the privacy settings were actually helpful—notably, the ability to set privacy options for individual posts—the overall bias was troubling. As an analysis by the Electronic Frontier Foundation concluded, the new settings "push Facebook users to publicly share even more information than before. Even worse, the changes will actually reduce the amount of control that users have over some of their personal data."

Facebook's extremely smart leaders know perfectly well that the majority of users are likely to accept these suggestions. Most people say yes to whatever the default settings are in any application, even though we should always be wary of the defaults, precisely for reasons like this.

I wasn't very happy with my Facebook situation in any case. Early on, I said yes to just about everyone who asked me to "friend" them, including people barely knew and some I didn't know at all.

The privacy changes—and my continuing uncertainty about what I was sharing, given the still-large number of pages you have to look at to modify your settings—made me realize I'd rather take fewer chances. So I made a fairly drastic change.

I deleted my account. Then I started a new one.

Actually, I scheduled the old one for deletion, which is all Facebook allowed. The company figures, perhaps correctly, that some people will have made this decision rashly and wants to give them a chance to reconsider. And it's clearly in Facebook's business interest to minimize the number of cancellations.

It wasn't easy to figure out how to delete the account, which no doubt is part of the company's strategy, too. If you go to the Settings page, the only option offered is to "deactivate," not delete.

But a little searching on the site turns up a Facebook Group called "How to permanently delete your Facebook account" (with more than 70,000 members at the time of this writing)—which in turn reveals an actual delete-account form located at still another Web address that Facebook doesn't reveal in any prominent way, if at all.

After creating my new account, I checked the default privacy settings. They're pretty un-private, in my view, sharing way too much with people you don't know. I systematically went through the various screens—Facebook makes this chore both annoying and obscure—to ratchet down the settings to something I can live with.

We all know Facebook profits from exposing to search engines and advertisers the largest possible number of pages by the largest number of people willing to create stuff and make it public. Marketers drool at the prospects Facebook offers, and Facebook's entirely rational goal is to make profits in almost any way it can. What's in the corporate interest, however, doesn't necessarily match what's in my interest, or yours.

So I'm still at facebook.com/dangillmor—though my real Web home base is dangillmor.com, as we'll discuss in the next chapter—but now I have just a small selection of Facebook friends. I'll be adding more, but not in any hasty way.

Freedom to Tinker: Who Owns Your iPhone, Anyway?

You may think you own the device you bought last week from a retailer. But it is increasingly the case that what you own is only the hardware; you don't own the right to use it the way you want to use it, even for entirely legal purposes.

The consequences of this reality have been researched deeply by Jonathan Zittrain, a Harvard law professor, friend and colleague from when I was a fellow at the Berkman Center for Internet & Society. He is also the author of *The Future of the Internet—and How to Stop It*. Zittrain describes a potential future in which the very qualities that have made the Internet so valuable—notably, its openness to innovation by everybody—are in danger. Whereas the personal computer and the early Internet were a wide-open collection of technologies on which anyone could build software and services, now governments and the technology and media industries increasingly want to clamp down on your freedoms. Zittrain writes:

> A lockdown on PCs and a corresponding rise of tethered appliances [like the iPhone] will eliminate what today we take for granted: a world where mainstream technology can be influenced, even revolutionized, out of left field. Stopping this future depends on some wisely developed and implemented locks, along with new technologies and a community ethos that secures the keys to those locks among groups with shared norms and a sense of public purpose, rather than in the hands of a single gatekeeping entity, whether public or private.

The iPhone and iPad are the best examples yet of a controlled ecosystem, and not just because you have to tether them to a PC or Mac in order to fully manage the music, songs, apps and other files on these (admittedly lovely) devices. With the Macintosh computer, Apple built an essentially open ecosystem for software developers. Anyone could write and sell (or give away) software for the Mac, and still can, just as they can for Windows and Linux and other computer operating systems. But with the iPhone and the iPad, Apple expanded on its experience with the iTunes Music Store, creating a system for retailing applications designed for these devices—but only if Apple has approved them. The number of applications available is said to exceed 300,000, but there are well-documented horror stories featuring Apple's refusal, often on mysterious grounds, to allow specific applications to be sold or even given away to iPhone/iPad users.

You can still create what you want on the Web, and iPhone users can still find it via the device's Safari browser—but sorry, no videos using Adobe's Flash player that runs most videos on desktop and laptop computers. Meanwhile, if you want your audience to experience your work in any way that uses the iPhone or iPad hardware to its fullest capabilities, you need Apple's permission to distribute the app that does this. And, then, if you get permission and charge for your application, or for any services you provide via your application, Apple insists on taking a cut of the money.

Google's Android mobile operating system is more open, but the company's real customers for it are the mobile carriers—AT&T, Verizon, etc.—that are busy locking down what their customers can do with their devices. Control-freakery is endemic, and dangerous.

Amazon, a company in which I own some stock, has locked down its Kindle platform, too. The Kindle is the most popular e-reader by far, and while I own one I'm extremely unhappy about Amazon's hard-nosed insistence that it can control your Kindle. The company was appropriately embarrassed (and had to pay out a court settlement) for remotely <u>deleting</u> several books by George Orwell, including *1984*—oh, the irony—from the Kindles of people who'd bought the editions from what turned out to be a publisher that was unauthorized to sell them. While Amazon apologized for its actions, it didn't say what would happen if some judge or government agency ordered it to remove books or other content from the devices in the future.

This is not just about your right to read and use media as you wish. It is also about the way you will be able to make available what you create in the future. If you believe in freedom of speech, and see mediactivity's value to our lives, our culture and our democracy, you should be deeply alarmed by the trends we're seeing.

Open Networks

Apple's attitude is alarming enough, but the company is a freedom fighter compared with the major telecommunications companies. Brazen control freaks, they don't have enough competitors—as Apple still does—to give them the slightest concern for the independent desires of their customers.

In *We the Media* I wrote that we are heading into a world with only one, two or at most three broadband telecommunications providers serving any given geographical community. I asked, back in 2004:

> Should giant telecommunications companies—namely cable and local phone providers—have vertical control over everything from the data transport to the content itself? For example, as I was writing this book, Comcast, the cable monopoly in my area, was trying to buy Disney. The attempt failed. If this happened, Comcast could have decided to deliver Disney's content online more quickly than someone else's, discriminating on the basis of financial considerations. Such a regime would have been a disaster for the unimpeded flow of information. We should insist on a more horizontal system, in which the owner of the pipe is obliged to provide interconnections to competing services. Unfortunately, today's regulatory and political power brokers lean in the wrong direction.

Late in 2009, Comcast announced it was buying NBC Universal, one of the biggest "content" companies on the planet. It's time to worry, and to act.

What's at stake? Free-speech activists have worried for years about the corporate consolidation of mass media. In the era when mass media held nearly total sway, that was a reasonable fear. And to the extent that Big Media holds onto its huge audiences, it's still a legitimate issue.

But now we face a consolidation that dwarfs anything contemplated before: the "broadband" oligopoly's increasing control over what we can do with our media. The cable and phone giants are determined to decide what bits get delivered in what order, at what speed and at what time—if at all—to the people who want them. We are heading toward a level of media control that, if the telecom companies succeed in achieving it, will threaten every bit of the work I and many others have been doing for the past decade—not to mention our mediactive future.

What do these companies want? Their plain goal is to turn the Internet into something that resembles cable television, where they decide which channels you need and which you'll pay extra to get (in this case, penalizing you if you want your own choice of feeds, videos and the like at the same speed you get their preferred ones).

What's especially galling is the telecom companies' claims that they have a right to control your choices because the networks are entirely their own property. Historically, they got this property via monopoly deals with local governments, allowing them to tear up streets and claim rights of way in a system that no new competitor can possibly duplicate. Serious competition, except in a tiny number of places, is unlikely, barring some advances in mobile technology that are more theoretical than imminent.

The mobile carriers are, if anything, even more restrictive. They have a reason at the moment, given the limited capacity of their networks. But in moves that can't remotely be blamed on network availability, they have curtailed all kinds of activities that they deem contrary to their own interests: notably, preventing Internet-based voice applications from competing. Alarmingly, Google—once a prime mover for "network neutrality," the term open-network advocates use to describe the kinds of networks we need—has joined with Verizon in a public statement all but abandoning the principle for mobile networks.

The Federal Communications Commission has been looking at network neutrality, but in the end Congress will decide this, and Congress has been a pawn of the telecom industry for too long. You should care about your ability to read and watch what you want, and the ability of others to read or watch what you create, in a fair marketplace. And if you do care, you should tell the people who represent you in the U.S. House and Senate that you do, and why.

Copyrights and Takedowns

One reason network providers are clamping down is pressure from the copyright cartel composed of the Hollywood movie studios and the big music recording companies. They call copyright infringement by a different name—"piracy"—and they've relentlessly protected their mass media content from anyone who might use it in any unauthorized way.

You have rights, as a consumer and a mediactive creator, as part of the broader "fair use" doctrine. For example, you can make personal backup copies of the music you buy. You also have the right to use other people's work in limited ways to create new works. (The key word there is "limited"—don't cut and paste large parts of other people's work, period; and always, always credit the creator whose material you do quote or reuse.)

The cartel says it has nothing against fair use, but the policies it advocates would effectively do away with that right and many others. Its members want to tell you when you can copy anything for any reason. This is an attack on journalism, among other things (including scholarship).

The more we need permission to use other peoples' work, the less building we'll all do on what's come before. Yet quoting is at the heart of cultural and scientific progress.

This doesn't mean we should do away with copyright. I'm a big believer in its proper uses, which include balancing the incentive to create with the public's right to use what others have created in new ways.

One of the heartening developments in recent years has been the growth of Creative Commons, an organization that helps people create and use material under a system that shares the creators' rights with the general public in ways that promote further creative development. This book, like my last one, is published under a Creative Commons license permitting you to freely copy it for non-commercial purposes, and to build on what you find in new works provided that you give full attribution and release any new works based on this one under the same terms.

Copyright holders have a powerful weapon online: the "takedown notice" they can send to a site where, they allege, someone has posted works in an infringing way. If the site owners put up the material themselves, they are legally liable (although usually the copyright holder asks for no punishment beyond having the content removed). If a site user posted the material, the site host can avoid legal trouble by complying with the takedown notice. If whoever posted it challenges the notice, saying the material is not infringing, the content goes back up, and the copyright holder is then required to litigate if he or she wants to force the issue.

It sounds like a good system, but in practice, copyright holders have abused it. If the person being threatened with a lawsuit has the means to fight back, though, the plaintiffs can be held financially liable for "abusive" claims—as Diebold, a company that sold electronic voting machines, did when it "knowingly misrepresented that online commentators, including IndyMedia and two Swarthmore college students, had infringed the company's copyrights." In that case, Diebold was <u>sued</u> successfully by the Electronic Frontier Foundation and had to pay $125,000 in damages and fees.

Some Legal Resources

The <u>Citizen Media Law Project</u> (CMLP) is based at Harvard University's Law School and the Berkman Center for Internet & Society. I'm biased toward this project, because I co-founded it and blog occasionally on the CMLP website. The project features resources ranging from a database of legal threats to, most recently, the <u>Online Media Legal Network</u>, which "connects lawyers from across the country with online journalists and digital media creators who need legal help."

The Electronic Frontier Foundation, a non-profit based in San Francisco, works to preserve our liberties in the technology and cyberspace spheres. I also have some bias here: In 2002 the EFF honored me with one of its annual Pioneer <u>awards</u>, and I'm friendly with the organization's founders, <u>John Perry Barlow</u>, <u>John Gilmore</u> and <u>Mitch Kapor</u>. (I've also been a financial donor to the EFF, and I urge you to do the same.)

There's an enormous amount of useful material at the CMLP and EFF websites. I'd strongly suggest that you look around, especially if you have any questions about what you might encounter as a creator—or host—of online content. They aren't the only excellent resources, and we'll list many other sources on the Mediactive website as well.

Defamation and Other Risks

What is defamation? <u>According to the EFF</u>:

> Generally, defamation is a false and unprivileged statement of fact that is harmful to someone's reputation, and published

"with fault," meaning as a result of negligence or malice. State laws often define defamation in specific ways. Libel is a written defamation; slander is a spoken defamation.

You are not exempt from laws just because you say things online. If you libel people on your blog or in a comment on someone else's blog, they can sue you and win.

If you follow the principles in Chapter 4, you're unlikely to libel anyone. Does that mean you'll be immune from being sued? Unfortunately, no.

Anyone can sue anyone else for the cost of filing a court fee, and judges rarely punish people for filing lawsuits they can't win (even if they probably know they can't). Moreover, whereas in some countries, such as the United Kingdom, libel defendants have to prove that what they've said was true, in the U.S. the plaintiff has to show that it was false (and public figures additionally have to prove that the statements were made maliciously or with indifference to the truth).

Since defamation and libel do happen for real, and can hurt people, you should be careful about what you say online, just as you would if you were giving a speech. From the principles laid out in Chapter 5, it should be obvious that you need to be accurate when you say something negative about somebody. I don't say this to scare you away from holding up the light to wrongdoing. Getting incontrovertible evidence of your claims and being fair to the people you criticize will be your best insurance against a libel lawsuit—but no amount of care is foolproof.

Defending yourself, even if you're absolutely in the right, is expensive. So learn ahead of time ways to avoid legal risk, even if you can't prevent it entirely. The EFF has an excellent Legal Guide for Bloggers. Here are several other valuable resources:

- The Knight Citizen News Network's "Top 10 Rules for Limiting Your Legal Risk": A set of concepts and solid advice for minimizing the risk you expose yourself to.

- The Citizen Media Law Project's Legal Guide: This increasingly comprehensive guide has an enormous amount of content dealing with individual states. One of the best features is a "decision tree" that helps you decide whether you need separate insurance for defamation and other legal risks beyond what you may already have in your homeowner's or renter's policy.

- Online Media Law: The Basics for Bloggers and Other Online Publishers. This is a multimedia course offered via the Poynter

Institute's News University. Once you pass it you may be eligible to buy specially priced insurance.

According to Kimberley Isbell, an attorney with the Harvard project and a Berkman Center Fellow, what kinds of issues you cover and how you do it determines the level of risk: Applying basic journalistic standards, such as accuracy and fairness, reduces the risk. Isbell also stresses the importance of being careful in how you use other people's work, to avoid copyright troubles.

Not all the news is scary in this arena. If you or your organization host an online conversation, you benefit from one of the most positive parts of Congress's 1996 telecommunications overhaul: an exemption from defamation and similar claims. This exception does not extend to the person doing the defamation. This protection for site owners has done incalculable good for freedom of speech.

Photographers, Stand Your Ground

One of the most pernicious escalations against media creators in recent years has been the war on photography in public places. Again and again, we hear how overzealous law-enforcement people—and private security guards—have challenged people who are doing nothing more than taking pictures in public places. They claim to be preventing terrorism, but the evidence for this is at best thin.

A number of websites have sprung up to catalog and protest infringements on our rights to take pictures and videos. One of the best is called, unsurprisingly, "War on Photography," and it's full of depressingly familiar tales of harassment by officious transit workers, police officers, and security guards, among others.

The U.S. has nothing, in this regard, on the police-state tactics that become more obnoxious every year in the nation that gave us the Magna Carta: the United Kingdom. The horror stories there are enough to make you leave your camera home on a tourism visit, or, perhaps more wisely, visit a less paranoid nation.

Security expert Bruce Schneier is among the many who point out the futility, not to mention almost pure inanity, of this kind of official behavior. He urges us all to stand up for our rights:

> Fear aside, there aren't many legal restrictions on what you can photograph from a public place that's already in public view. If you're harassed, it's almost certainly a law enforcement official, public or private, acting way beyond his authority.

There's nothing in any post-9/11 law that restricts your right to photograph.

This is worth fighting. Search "photographer rights" on Google and download one of the several wallet documents that can help you if you get harassed; I found one for the UK, US, and Australia. Don't cede your right to photograph in public. Don't propagate the terrorist photographer story. Remind them that prohibiting photography was something we used to ridicule about the USSR. Eventually sanity will be restored, but it may take a while.

Freedom of Information: Public Records

One of the most important initiatives in recent decades has been the opening up of government records to public inspection. Although the U.S. federal government went into reverse on open records during the Bush administration, the trend at the federal and state level, and increasingly around the globe, is toward more openness and access.

When you request government records, keep this in mind:

1. You don't need to give a reason for your request. It's your business, not theirs, why you want to see public documents.
2. You should be as specific as possible about what you want. Overly broad document or data requests don't help you or your search.
3. Be persistent. Officials may turn you down the first time (and in my experience as a journalist, they often did), just to see if you're serious.

You can find a wealth of online resources on open records laws, state and federal. One is the National Freedom of Information Coalition, which sees its role as protecting the people's right to oversee their government.

In early 2010, the coalition won a $2 million grant to launch a freedom of information fund to help litigate state and local denials of open-records requests by citizens. This underscored the difficult side of open-records laws: dealing with recalcitrant officials who don't care what the law says. (I'm on the board of the First Amendment Coalition, a California-based nonprofit that litigates such requests.)

Public documents these days include data from databases, not just paper documents. In Chapter 10 I'll discuss some ways we can use that data to help create what is being called "Government 2.0."

Shield Laws

Apple isn't just control-freakish with its hardware. It's one of the most secretive companies in the world. In 2004, claiming trade secrets had been violated, Apple Inc. sued several internal "John Does"—employees who'd leaked product information to several websites—and demanded that the sites turn over details on where they had gotten the information. At the request of lawyers working for those sites (I was not paid), I declared in legal documents that in my expert opinion the sites were doing a form of journalism protected under California law. Several courts agreed, and the online journalists were not required to turn over the information.

California is one of many states with shield laws for journalists and confidential sources. Importantly, in the Apple case, the courts understood that even if the websites weren't doing traditional journalism, it was journalism nonetheless.

As of this writing, we still don't have a federal shield law, though one is making its way through Congress. But when and if it does pass, I hope it will protect journalism, in whatever form that takes—not the people we call journalists.

Having said all this about shield laws, I want to stress again that anonymous sources make me queasy. You may someday need to shield someone from harmful exposure, but you will be exposing yourself to challenges from common-sense readers who ask why your source didn't have the courage to speak on the record.

Overreach by Prosecutors

If you are honorable, you're almost certainly free from the risk of what follows. But when the laws get twisted to take down someone everyone dislikes, that's when we should all pay attention to our own freedoms.

In particular, when public officials start talking about "protecting the children," you may be hearing the standard code words for whacking civil liberties—and in the Internet age, core liberties such as free speech are in jeopardy.

The ugly case of Lori Drew is one example. Drew's daughter was involved in a conflict with Megan Meier, a teenage neighbor. Drew and several other people created a bogus MySpace account for a fictitious teenaged boy who wooed and then rejected Meier. Soon after, Meier committed suicide at her suburban St. Louis home. One thing is absolutely clear in this sordid case: Drew and her helpers in this sleazy scheme were heartless, and have been justly pilloried for their acts. But was this a prosecutable offence?

Officials in Missouri had no cause for criminal action because no state law fit the case. But federal prosecutors hauled Drew off to Los Angeles, headquarters of MySpace, and tried her for violating a federal law, the Computer Fraud and Abuse Act (CFAA), which had been used in the past to go after hackers who'd plundered others' computers for financial gain. Using a computer, prosecutors said, Drew had:

> [I]ntentionally accessed and caused to be accessed a computer used in interstate commerce, namely, the MySpace servers located in Los Angeles County, California, within the Central District of California, without authorization and in excess of authorized access, and, by means of interstate commerce obtained and caused to be obtained information from that computer to further tortious acts, namely intentional infliction of emotional distress on [Meier].

As the Citizen Media Law Project's Matt Sanchez explained, Drew's alleged crime was, boiled down to the actual law as opposed to the emotional element of the case, "nothing other than failing to submit 'truthful and accurate' registration information when creating a MySpace profile. She would have been no less liable for misstating her height."

Think about this. When using online registration systems, have you always, without exception, given utterly accurate information?

A jury acquitted Drew on a felony charge but found her guilty on a less-serious misdemeanor violation of the CFAA. But the judge overturned even that; as he explained in his ruling, allowing Drew's verdict to stand would have made everyone who's ever violated a terms of service agreement, no matter how minor the violation, guilty of a crime as well.

The prosecutor, Thomas P. O'Brien, didn't care. As Wired News reported, he was proud of himself. Sure, he said, using the CFAA was "a risk," but his office "will always take risks on behalf of children."

The larger risk was, in fact, to liberty. O'Brien's willingness to twist a law to serve even a well-meaning end deserves contempt, not praise, because he's supposed to know better. We are fortunate that the judge rescued the rest of us—not just the despicable Drew—from a prosecutor whose legal theories would have made criminals of just about everyone who has ever signed up for just about anything online.

Can the law handle a case like Drew's? Or what about the September 2010 suicide of a Rutgers University student who jumped off the George Washington Bridge after a video of him and a male friend having sex was posted online? Two fellow students were charged with invasion of privacy.

Harvard law professor John Palfrey—a friend and former colleague of mine when I was a Fellow at the Berkman Center, where he was executive director—advises caution. He wrote in the *New York Times* of the Rutgers case and a Massachusetts suicide also attributed to cyber-bullying:

> In using the law to address this problem, we need first to examine whether the law is sufficient in this new hybrid online-offline environment to discourage this kind of behavior and whether we are acting in a just manner with respect to those who are harmed and those who do the harm. Second, we need to ask whether our law enforcement officials have the support they need to get the job done.

Most states have a series of laws that address criminal harassment, whether it happens online or offline. These laws ordinarily permit both criminal enforcement by the state and civil lawsuits. One challenge associated with these laws is to not criminalize behavior that amounts to ordinary teenager-to-teenager nastiness while drawing a line well before the kinds of behavior that might lead to a teenager's suicide.

Again, anyone who is honorable isn't going to do this kind of thing. Still, we need to be aware of so-called fixes to essentially moral problems—fixes that could make it harder for everyone to participate in our new collaborative environment.

Norms and Customs

Indeed, the cases I've described weren't, in the end, only about law. They also had everything to do with the norms, or customs, we should consider as we work, play and collaborate in a digital mediasphere.

In previous chapters we've considered how we should react to things we find online, especially derogatory and even hateful speech, and how we should behave ourselves in our speech. I want to give these issues extra emphasis here.

It should go without saying that people shouldn't use our new media tools for cruel purposes. Given that some will, what kinds of norms can we encourage so that the targets of cruelty can either respond or, better yet, learn to ignore the attacks?

Telling our children to grow thicker skins is, of course, not going to get us very far, and we don't want to create a generation of purely cynical adults. But social-media training needs to include the digital-age versions of cautions we've long suggested to children, such as the admonition not to get into a car with an adult who's a stranger. Again, trust depends in large part on what we can verify, or what we've learned, though our own experience and the advice of others, to trust.

Words Come Back

My friend and Arizona State University colleague Tim McGuire says, "The fact is one stupid mistake when you are 19 today can kill your future."

That's true—today, anyway, as we learn that what we do online can often be rediscovered years later.

So when President Obama advised the Virginia student with political aspirations to watch what he posted on Facebook, he was being sensible, given the current climate.But if the president's advice turns out to have long-term validity, we are in some trouble as a society.

Young people make mistakes and do stupid things. (So do older people, of course. Meanwhile, my generation's youthful stupidities are mostly lost in the mists of time, unpreserved on a hard disk somewhere in the digital cloud.) But I hope it doesn't follow, as the president suggested, that posting "weird" things on the Web in blogs, social networks and the like should be an automatic turnoff or disqualification for a responsible job later in life. The notion of punishing someone decades later for what he or she said or did as a teenager or college student isn't just wrong. It's dangerous.

We're going to have to cut each other some slack. There's no alternative.

A journalism student of mine once asked if it was advisable to have a personal blog and, if so, to be outspoken on it. He'd apparently been warned that it could put a crimp in his future journalism career plans.

I can't say how others would react. I do know that if I were hiring someone today I'd want to know what (not if) he or she posted online, not to find disqualifying factors but to see if that person had interesting things to say. I'd take for granted that I might find some things that were risqué or inappropriate for my current world. I'd expect to find things that would be "unjournalistic" in some ways, such as outspoken or foolish (or both) views on important people and issues. But I'd also remember my own ability, if not tendency, to be an idiot when I was that age. And I'd discount appropriately.

This is all about giving people what my friend Esther Dyson, a technology investor and seer, has called a "statute of limitations on stupidity." If our norms don't bend so that we can all start cutting each other more slack in this increasingly transparent society, we'll only promote drones—the least imaginative, dullest people—into positions of authority. Now that's really scary.

We're making progress—probably more than Obama gives us credit for. Recall that it was impossible for a Catholic to be president until John F. Kennedy was elected. It was impossible for a divorced person to be elected until Ronald Reagan won. It was impossible for a former pot smoker to be president until Bill Clinton (who bizarrely claimed not to have inhaled) got elected. George W. Bush acknowledged having been a dissolute drunk until he was 40. And so on.

Making These Judgments Is Neither Clear nor Simple

Virginia Gov. Robert McDonnell took hits during his 2009 campaign for the office when a 20-year-old master's thesis came to light. In that document he denounced programs that encouraged women to work outside the home and said working women were bad for families. He wanted voters to ignore all this and concentrate on what he said were his current positions.

McDonnell deserved some slack, too, but he wrote the thesis when he was in his mid-30s, not his early 20s or adolescence. His record as a legislator since then has been extremely conservative, as well. What he said two decades ago is obviously more relevant, given the circumstances, than what a student posts on a high-school Facebook page today. Still, he won the election.

Sometime in the foreseeable future, we'll elect a president who had a blog or Facebook wall or MySpace page when she was a teenager or a college student. By the standards of today, such a person would be utterly disqualified for any serious political job. But if we adapt as I believe we'll have to, we'll have grown as a society; we'll have become not just more tolerant of flaws, but more understanding that we all have feet of clay in some respect. We'll elect her anyway, because we'll realize that the person she has become—and how that happened—is what counts.

How will her peers know all this? They'll have figured it out for themselves, but they'll have had some help, too. They'll have been taught, from an early age.

In the next chapter, we'll see who the teachers should be.

Chapter 10

Teaching and Learning Mediactivity

We run all kinds of deficits in our society. We spend money we don't have, at every level of society, sinking ourselves into perhaps unpayable debt for the long run. We invest too little and speculate too much, and our political class caters to a national refusal to face up to long-term realities.

We've been running a similar deficit in critical thinking. We regiment children instead of helping them to be creative, teaching them to take standardized tests instead of helping them think for themselves. In too many school districts, teaching critical thinking would be denounced as a dangerous experiment.

It's not dangerous at all. It's entirely American to challenge authority. But skepticism shouldn't become pure cynicism that we drape over everything we see. It should motivate us to seek out the best evidence, and learn from what we discover.

We need to teach our kids how to be mediactive in a media-saturated world. But they're not the only ones who need instruction; adults who are not digital natives have plenty to learn, while modern youths who think they know the media terrain often can't (or don't bother to) distinguish different levels of trustworthy information in the midst of their forum-hopping. For all of us, no matter our age, mediactivity is a lifetime practice, a collection of principles and skills that we keep learning and tweaking, in part because technology and our societal norms have a way of changing, too.

Why should we do this? Because democratized media is part of democracy, and democracy is about more than simply voting. It is about participation as citizens. Participating in media is a step toward being participants in a broader way, which works, in the end, only when we know what we're talking about; citizenship is not an exercise in demagoguery with your neighbors as props, but rather is about persuading and working with them—and perhaps being persuaded by them.

Those deeply committed to mediactivism will not only consume news wisely and create materials that help their communities, but will always be on the lookout for ways to help others become mediactive and sharpen their own skills.

Media Literacy

I've avoided the expression "media literacy" in this book for one major reason: It feels like terminology from an older era, and what media literacy has meant in the past doesn't map so well to the future. Yet the fundamental concept remains valuable, even if it needs updating.

When I said this in a blog posting in late 2008, I got some pushback from one of the leaders in the field, Renee Hobbs, a professor at Temple University and head of the school's exemplary Media Education Lab. When I referred to media literacy—as an expression, as opposed to a concept—as "quaint to the point of irrelevance," she chided me (fairly) for dissing my allies, adding:

> We've been debating terms for this concept for 15 years. Everybody and his brother has a different name for it: "digital literacy," "information literacy" and "cyberliteracy" just to name a few. Thanks for at least using the right term: media literacy.

Participation is by definition and tradition a vital part of any literacy; yet for me the term "media literacy" has taken on connotations mostly of smarter consumption. So the reason I look for new language is to emphasize the participation that's now so integral to media in a grassroots-enabled world.

Technology—the Internet, blogs and microblogging, digital photography and video, high-speed networks and more—has changed the media landscape radically in recent years. And we've adopted technology at an amazing pace. From all over the landscape, people once relegated to observing from their couches have flocked to the new media, and these days the asides and comments of friends, followers and the followed often turn out to be just as important as the reports from professional journalists.

Whatever we call it, we agree that an active approach to reading the news is essential.

Media literacy has had several major threads over the past century. One is academic: the creation of an almost institutional system based on research and school-based instruction. Another has roots in political activism. Both of these threads—and a host of related ideas, such as "digital citizenship" and "critical literacy," to mention just two of the many competing expressions in the field—are a good starting point for more contemporary efforts.

Until recently, many activists in the media literacy movement, notably the left-of-center folks, were somewhat preoccupied with the still-real dangers of corporate media consolidation. Media critics and reformers on the political left and right have found too little common ground. One of the few places they have started to collaborate is network neutrality, which activists on many sides have finally realized is key to their own futures—though here we find a tendency of people on the right to favor corporate interests ahead of the public interest.

Media literacy advocates of all stripes, inside and outside academia, have moved toward participation. We all need to push this much further. Mediactivism is, above all, about *doing* things: action and participation.

That won't end what Hobbs and Amy Jensen of Brigham Young University described, in the Journal of Media Literacy Education, as "tensions between educators, activists, artists, civic, political, governmental, media, and business leaders regarding the differing roles and functions" of media literacy education. But I especially like the way the researchers I've cited celebrate the complexity—created by the various social and political perspectives they see—of what they call our "journey to empowerment."

Empowerment takes more than mere knowledge; we need to translate what we know into action. Whether we call it media literacy, news literacy, mediactivism or anything else, above all, we need to push participation, not as a chore but as something satisfying and vital.

We Teach, We Learn, We Do

We can't act, however, until we understand why we should, and how. Who should lead in the lifelong mediactivity process of learning and participation? Everyone, really. Anyone lucky enough to have the access we all have to the world's best ideas and knowledge, plus the education to understand and talk coherently about them, can reach out to others.

The primary guides to critical thinking should be the ones you'd expect—parents, friends, schools and institutions devoted to learning outside of the education system—plus perhaps one group you might not expect. That's the journalists themselves, who should have been among the leading proponents of these skills and principles but, for the most part, haven't bothered.

Schools

Media literacy's rise in American education has long roots. Some scholars credit in particular the work of a Jesuit priest, the late John Culkin (1928–1993). Founder of the now-defunct Center for Understanding Media, based in New York, Culkin wanted teachers to think in ways they hadn't contemplated before. In a biographical essay, Kate Moody, one of the early practitioners of Culkin's notions, wrote:

> He believed that if teachers understood the function of media in culture, they could use that awareness to help young people become better learners. By the late 1960s there was more information outside the classroom than in it, due to the pervasiveness of film and TV. Much of the information was really misinformation, so that "separating the signal from the noise" became a necessary task. It was important for educators to grapple with this disparity between information levels outside and inside the school. That meant dealing with the full spectrum of materials to which pupils were exposed outside and to help them deal with it critically and reflectively, rather than with the passivity that had come to be associated with habitual TV viewing.

Culkin and his allies pushed hard to incorporate media skills and understanding into the curriculum. They had some success over the past half-century; media literacy has become a widely known concept, practiced in some schools and promoted by a variety of people and organizations worried about mass media's influence.

In recent years their successors have looked at the digital sphere and realized they had to confront new and even more difficult issues—especially the diffusion of sources beyond what once had been a relatively few mass media organizations. Where television was once the major concern, now we have to understand digital media and incorporate them into a much more complex equation.

According to Hobbs, to the extent that media literacy is taught in the K–12 environment, it tends to be integrated into specific subject areas—health, for example—and mostly in middle schools. Statistics are thin on its penetration in America's classrooms; Hobbs doubts that even 30 percent of U.S. students are exposed to it in any formal way. But she's certain, based on her own observations and the publishing of more dissertations on the topic, that interest is growing.

There's no national curriculum or standardized lesson plans in the area of media literacy—and for good reason, Hobbs says. U.S. public education is decentralized, and media are changing so fast that wise teachers need to constantly update what they're teaching. Further diminishing the possibility of standards, according to Hobbs, is that the best teachers are incorporating media-creation skills, not just tips on smarter consumption, into their offerings.

Can schools ever be the most important place for media literacy education? I have my doubts, in part because this is so much about teaching kids to be critical thinkers. Look around, and consider the political climate. I'll say it again: In many parts of America, a teacher who tried to do this would be branded as a dangerous radical.

Some media literacy advocates have all but given up on schools. Hobbs definitely hasn't. She told me:

> I have a lot of respect for teachers. Schools can be repressive. They're designed to be culturally conservative. Yet good teachers, who are everywhere, know that learning happens only when you make a connection between the learner and the competencies.

Sidebar: danah boyd on Teachers and Media Literacy

Social media researcher danah boyd, who served on the Knight Commission on the Information Needs of Communities in a Democracy, has been studying young people's adoption of digital media. Her perspective on media literacy and schools is cogent. As she told me:

> I sit down with teachers in this country and my heart breaks for them, because they've gotten to a world where they have so many standards that they have to measure up to, where they don't feel like they're teachers anymore. They don't feel like they're actually teaching kids to think. And many of them want to teach kids to think.

> They may or may not have the skills to do so, and that's a whole separate ball of wax. But a lot of them really want to give young people the skills, which include critical thinking, to move forward as adults. They want to teach them how to think about the world at large...

English education used to be a core place of critical thinking. Read *To Kill a Mockingbird* and start deconstructing it. Now it's like, "Can you prove that you remember the following seven things from the book?"

Some of the hardest [teaching] jobs these days are trying to teach the most privileged kids in this country, because a lot of those teachers want to push back at the expectations that the kids bring into the classroom. But that unfortunately means pushing back at the expectations of the parents. And that's a lot harder. And that's actually a space where I worry much more for engaging in destructive activities.

I actually think there's a lot more opportunity though for kids who are traditionally underprivileged to really be given critical thinking skills that will help them in the workforce and as they go forward. So if we just start with the underprivileged kids, I'm okay with that.

Parents

Teachers in schools can only go so far. Parents are the first educators of children in any case, and raising children for the world we will live in will surely mean helping them become adaptable in their intellectual habits.

The Internet has been a boon for parents looking for help. You can find any number of excellent online resources for helping your children understand media. The PBS Parents website, for example, has a thorough archive of articles, videos and more on the topic. (And, as usual, we'll point to a bunch of others on the Mediactive website, mediactive.com.)

But I also want to make a different kind of pitch to parents. As I've said again and again, tactics mean nothing without principles. Teach your kids skepticism, honesty, zeal to find the truth and the other principles in this book, and they'll find the rest of what they need naturally.

Friends and Colleagues

Remember the email I quoted in Chapter 1? It was an email forwarded from a colleague of mine, one of many such missives his father regularly sends him, informing the reader of several fairly amazing "facts" regarding America, Osama bin Laden and the September 11 attacks. My colleague wrote that he didn't have time to check further, though he was appropriately skeptical. I did visit Snopes.com to check it out, and learned that the email was a twisted series of lies, cloaked in some actual events that gave the lies a patina of reality. It was plainly designed to inflame, not inform.

The charges, which I won't detail again, have been making their way around the Net for some time. There's no doubt that lots of its intended readers believe every word, because they want to.

How should we respond when friends and colleagues forward such things? I believe we all have a duty to do more than simply shrug and delete them. At the very least I'd urge a friend who forwarded me a note like this to be skeptical and check it out, and I'd also encourage him to tell whoever sent it to him to do the same. In this case I let my colleague know what I'd found, and I hope he let his father know. Whether it went back beyond that, I'll never know—but it should have.

We have a special duty to tell people we've been wrong when we give them information that turns out to be false. They'll appreciate the correction, and trust us more in the end.

Journalists

In June 2009, the *New Yorker* ran a story about America's health-care crisis. The reporter, Atul Gawande, did something remarkable. He'd discovered dramatic differences between health-care costs in two U.S. communities, and he sought to explain why one place spent vastly more per capita than the other, yet had a significantly poorer overall health record. His article was, in part, an explanation of how he had done the journalistic detective work to figure out the reasons.

A little over a year earlier, National Public Radio had run a lengthy story called "Giant Pool of Money"—a program that asked the question too few journalists had been asking in previous years: namely, how it was that so many people who couldn't afford to make home-mortgage payments were getting the loans anyway. It was a masterpiece of investigative and explanatory journalism, and an essential part of the report was the explanation of how the journalists had discovered the information. Early in the show, co-reporter Alex Blumberg told listeners part of his thought process as he gathered information for the story:

> The thing that got me interested in all this was something called a NINA loan. Back when the housing crisis was still a housing bubble. A guy on the phone told me that a NINA loan stands for No Income, No Asset, as in, someone will lend you a bunch of money without first checking if you have any income or any assets. And it was an official, loan product.

Like, you could walk into a mortgage broker's office and they would say, well, we can give you a 30-year fixed rate, or we could put you in a NINA. He said there were lots of loans like this, where the bank didn't actually check your income, which I found confusing. It turns out even the people who got them found them confusing.

Both the NPR and the *New Yorker* pieces were examples of something that's been largely absent from the journalism craft, to its detriment: a recognition that media has a role in helping people develop critical thinking skills, and that journalists—explaining what they do and why—can be among the best teachers.

Traditional media have done a generally lousy job of this. They've been content to produce their products and (at least until recently) rake in the money, without much concern for helping audiences understand what journalists actually do when they do their jobs well.

I'm not talking here about gratuitous bragging, especially when there's little to brag about (which is all too often the case). But the better a news organization does its job in solid or superlative ways, the more important it may be to let the audience in on the hows and whys. The result might include more support and funds from the community for professional journalists. But for the future of journalism, the more important outcome would be a greater appreciation of why everybody needs to do this work.

Brent Cunningham, in an article that originally appeared in the *Columbia Journalism Review*, offered sound advice:

[J]ournalism would need to begin to change the narrative about itself. It is a narrative that has been created by the press's own failures, its arrogance and shortsightedness, but also by a forty-year campaign by segments of the political right to vilify the press as a "liberal" cabal, and a more recent and less coordinated effort by elements on the left to portray it as a corporate stooge. Changing this narrative will not be easy. There is considerable hostility and distrust toward the mainstream news media, but some of it is the result of ignorance about what the press does and why. The partisan press-haters will always be with us, but the nascent News Literacy movement is attempting to rectify the pervasive ignorance about the values and methods of journalism—to instill in young citizens the importance of the best kinds of journalism, and how to distinguish it from the less-reliable, less-intellectually honest stuff that floods our information environment each day.

The "news literacy" genre, as noted by Cunningham, is indeed nascent, but it's growing in smart ways. One good example is the News Literacy Project, founded by Alan Miller, a former *Los Angeles Times* journalist. It brings working reporters and editors into schools to help students understand the (best) values of journalism, and put those values into practice.

This kind of thing should be routine, not a brave new experiment.

Media Skills and Civic Engagement

Some of the most promising work in mediactivsm has come via the Internet, using traditional and new institutions in wonderfully creative ways. No one knows more about the intersection of old and new than Henry Jenkins.

An author and professor, Jenkins ran the Comparative Media Studies program at the Massachusetts Institute of Technology before moving to the University of Southern California, where he is Provost's Professor of Communication, Journalism and Cinematic Arts. For decades he's been working on understanding the changes in media, and how they can spur civic engagement. He celebrates, among other developments, the fan clubs and comment sites that have sprung up around movies, television shows and pop musicians. He sees them as forms of social expression just as legitimate as conventional political commentary—and, moreover, as a bridge to greater political involvement.

We've moved ahead, Jenkins says, but not nearly far enough, "especially when we're talking about the educational culture, which is remarkably resistant to technology, resistant to new methods, and certainly resistant to ideas of critical citizenship." In a conversation, he continued:

> We know we've lost ground in terms of civics, instruction through schools, in terms of the ability of school newspapers to investigate and publish information, in terms of classroom discussions of public policy issues. Teachers are often straightjacketed and schools and students certainly are, where we're seeing bans on social network sites, on YouTube, all of the tools and platforms that are being used outside of school to foster a more participatory culture....

[Yet] if you go outside of school, if we look at the studies that are done pretty regularly by the Pew Center for Internet and American Life, they're finding 60–65% of American young people have produced media. A high percentage of American teens are involved in publishing some kind of blog or live journal online or participating in online forums.... Those kids who participate actively in game guilds and social networks and in networks in general are more likely to take the next step and be involved with the political activities of their local or national community. There is a direct connection that we're starting to identify between participation in these kinds of cultural forums and participation in civic forums.

So outside of school we're seeing dramatic gains. Inside of school, there's a kind of no-fly zone that's preventing people from being able to fully engage with these new practices.

My father used to say, never let schooling get in the way of your education. And this may be one of those contexts where schools are getting in the way, in many cases, rather than facilitating the acquisition of the kind of citizenship skills that you and I are interested in.

Jenkins, through his own work and observations of other efforts, points to a host of intriguing projects, some organized and some organic—and most taking place outside the formal education system. Global Kids, based in New York, has done what its name suggests: bringing children from around the world together, in mostly virtual ways, to understand public policy at the local level, but in a global context.

He also points to the Harry Potter Alliance, which comes out of the "fandom" arena: fans of cultural works who discuss those works and, at some point, start collaborating on their own, using the skills they've developed as fans and applying them in wider realms, including the news. Harry Potter challenges authority. As Jenkins explains, Harry Potter's Alliance fans have "gone and said, 'Okay, what would Dumbledore's Army do in our time? Where is evil? What change can we bring about?' So they've got 50 chapters worldwide, 100,000 young people involved in struggles over human rights issues, both abroad and in the United States." This is exciting stuff.

Journalism Education's Opportunity

Accepting an <u>award</u> from Arizona State University's Walter Cronkite School for Journalism & Mass Communication in 2008, former <u>PBS NewsHour</u> host <u>Robert McNeil</u> <u>called</u> journalism education probably "the best general education that an American citizen can get" today.

Perhaps he was playing to his audience, at least to a degree. Many other kinds of undergraduate degree programs could lay claim to a similar value; a strong liberal arts degree, no matter what the major, has great merit. Still, there's no doubt that a journalism degree, done right, is an excellent foundation for a student's future in any field, not just media.

Even if McNeil overstated the case, his words should inspire journalism educators to ponder their role in a world where these programs' traditional reason for being is increasingly murky.

Our *raison d'etre* is open to question largely because the employment pipeline of the past, a progression leading from school to jobs in media and related industries, is (at best) in jeopardy. We're still turning out young graduates who go off to work in entry-level jobs, particularly in broadcasting—but where is their career path from there?

If traditional media have adapted fitfully to the collision of technology and media, journalism schools as a group may have been even slower to react to the huge shifts in the craft and its business practices. Only recently have they embraced digital technologies in their work with students who plan to enter traditional media. Too few are helping students understand that they may well have to invent their own jobs, much less helping them do so.

Yet journalism education could and should have a long and even prosperous life ahead—if its practitioners make some fundamental shifts, recognizing the realities of the 21st century.

In Chapter 8 I told you how I'd run a news organization. If I ran a journalism school, I would start with the same basic principles of honorable, high-quality journalism and mediactivism, and embed them at the core of everything else. If our students didn't understand and appreciate them, nothing else we did would matter very much.

With the principles as the foundation, we would, among many other things (the full list is on <u>mediactive.com</u>):

- Emphasize undergraduate journalism degrees as great liberal arts programs, perhaps even more valuable when viewed that way than as training for journalism careers. At the same time, we would focus graduate journalism studies on helping people with expertise in specific areas to be the best possible journalists in their fields.

- Encourage, and require in some cases, cross-disciplinary learning and doing. We'd create partnerships around the university, working with business, engineering/computer science, film, political science, law, design and many other programs. The goals would be both to develop our own projects and to be an essential community-wide resource for the future of local media.

- Teach students not just the basics of digital media but also the value of data and programming to their future work. This doesn't necessarily mean that they need to become programmers, but they absolutely need to know how to communicate with programmers. We'd also encourage computer science undergraduates to become journalism graduate students, so they can help create tomorrow's media.

- Require all students to learn basic statistics, survey research and fundamental scientific methodology. The inability of journalists to understand the math they encounter in their reading is one of journalism's—and society's—major flaws.

- Encourage a research agenda with deep connections to key media issues of today. More than ever, we need solid data and rigorous analysis. And translate faculty research into language average people can understand as opposed to the dense, even impenetrable, prose that's clear (if it really is) only to readers of academic journals.

- Require all journalism students to understand business concepts, especially those relating to media. This is not just to cure the longstanding ignorance of business issues in the craft, but also to recognize that today's students will be among the people who develop tomorrow's journalism business models. We'd discuss for-profit and not-for-profit methods, and look at advertising, marketing, social networking, and search-engine optimization, among many other elements.

- Make entrepreneurship a core part of journalism education. Arizona State University, where I work, is among several schools working on this, and the early experiments are gratifying. Several of our student projects have won funding. At City University of New York, Jeff Jarvis has received foundation funding for student projects to continue after the class is over, based on semester-ending competitive "pitches" to a judging panel of journalists and investors. We need to see more and more of these and other kinds of experiments.

- Persuade the president (or chancellor, or whatever the title) and trustees of the university that every student on the campus should learn journalism principles and skills before graduating, preferably during freshman year. At State University of New York's Stony Brook campus, the journalism school has been given a special mandate of exactly this kind. Howard Schneider, a former newspaper journalist who now is dean of Stony Brook's journalism school, won foundation funding to bring news literacy into the university's broader community, rather than only to those enrolled in journalism courses.

- Create a program of the same kind for people in the community, starting with teachers. Our goal would be to help schools across our geographical area bring mediactivism to every level of education—not just college, but also elementary, middle and high school. We would offer workshops, conferences and online training.

- Offer that program, or one like it, to concerned parents who feel overwhelmed by the media deluge themselves, to help turn them into better media consumers and to give them ways to help their children.

- Enlist another vital player in this effort: local media of all kinds, not just traditional media. Of course, as noted earlier, they should be making this a core part of their missions, given that their own credibility would rise if they helped people understand the principles and process of quality journalism. But we'd very much want to work with local new media organizations and individuals, too.

- Advise and train citizen journalists to understand and apply sound principles and best practices. They are going to be an essential part of the local journalism ecosystem, and we should reach out to show them how we can help.

- Augment local media with our own journalism. We train students to do journalism, after all, and their work should be widely available in the community, particularly when it fills in gaps left by the shrinking traditional media. At Arizona State, the <u>Cronkite News Service</u> provides all kinds of coverage of topics the local news organizations rarely cover, making our students' work available to those organizations.

All this suggests a considerably broader mission for journalism schools and programs than the one they've had in the past. It also suggests a huge opportunity for journalism schools. The need for this kind of training has never been greater. We're not the only ones who can do it, but we may be among the best equipped.

It's Everyone's Job

I hope we can all be learners, teachers and actors in mediactivism. The alternatives are a bit scary.

But to get to where we need to be, we also need better tools and techniques. In the next chapter we'll look at some of the possibilities.

Chapter 11

A Path to Tomorrow

So, what's missing?

As we move into the next generation of news and trustworthy information, what tools, techniques and business models need to be invented or perfected? What attitudes need to change in the general public? The list is too long for one book. But here are some of the most important "next steps" I can name right now:

- Create community-based networks of trust, using reputation as an essential component.

- Improve the tools of discovery and context, via aggregation and curation.

- Make the *topic* the primary focus of reporting, with dynamic "articles" that advance understanding through successive iterations as new information becomes available.

- Find and catalog the best ideas, techniques and tools, and then connect them with people who can bring them to a wider public.

- Get policy right on copyright and broadband. Eliminate subsidies, direct and indirect, that favor one type of media business over another.

- Develop payment systems that reward creators in all parts of the new media ecosystem.

- Make critical thinking and media literacy part of education's core curriculum.

- Do away with almost all journalism prizes, and bring the ones we want to keep into the 21st century.

- Work toward a national consensus on identity and accountability that encourages people to stand behind their words and to cut each other slack for past foolish acts and remarks.

- Continue the conversations.

Let me expand on some of these.

Topics and Baselines, Not Stories

If Steven Spielberg and other Hollywood folks can create directors' cuts of their movies, why can't journalists do the same—and more? Why can't they keep updating and improving their own published works?

Actually, they can, if they can get past the publication and broadcast models from the age of literally manufactured media, where the printed paper product or recording tape was the end of the process.

This is not just about newspapers or television and radio broadcasts. It's about books, too—in fact, about any of the media forms that are making the transition into the Digital Age. The Mediactive project represents my own attempt to put this notion and others into practice.

In life, we accrete knowledge. We learn a little more about things as we go along, and we factor that new information into a new understanding of the larger topics.

This model maps to the way the Web works. On the Web, the best explainers accrete audiences and authority, as they attract more and more readers and inbound links. As mediactive knowledge accretes, you'll find it in updates to the Mediactive website.

Because of its manufacturing model, traditional journalism has done things in a different way. The process has been to create a new story each time a bit more information about a person, topic or issue becomes available, and either to expect audiences to have enough background to understand why this turn of the screw matters or to add some background information that attempts to bring the reader/viewer/listener up to speed.

This is inefficient, both for the journalists and for the audience. But in an online world, we can easily do better.

One way to do it better: Create topic articles that are dynamic, with successive iterations adding (and subtracting) from the original as new information comes to light. This isn't a new idea—Wikipedia, after all, is precisely about this kind of approach, as I <u>noted</u> when I wrote about it in 2005—but it's gaining currency. (Jeff Jarvis put it especially well in his blog, BuzzMachine.com, when he <u>wrote</u>: "The building block of journalism is no longer the article." <u>Jay Rosen</u> and <u>Matt Thompson</u>, in a <u>panel</u> at the 2010 South by Southwest Interactive conference, greatly expanded on this notion when they examined what they called the "future of context," and created a <u>website</u> for it.)

Some models are already available. Consider Wikipedia, where every version of each article that is written—and I mean everything, down to the version where someone added a comma and hit the save button—is available to anyone who wants to see it. You can even compare edited versions side by side.

In the real world, how might this work?

Let's say I'm just starting to understand the role of financial tools called "collateralized debt obligations" (CDOs) in the 2008 financial meltdown. And suppose that the *New York Times* had done a detailed explainer of CDOs. (I can't find one, but perhaps it did.) Now comes the important part: Let's further suppose that the *Times* has been updating that article on the Web to reflect new events, in addition to writing current news stories (and archiving them next to the original) and creating a huge link directory. The newer stories have lots of new details, only the most central of which make it back into the updated original explainer.

The *Times* has actually gone part of the way in this direction. Under the umbrella of <u>"Times Topics"</u> you'll find a huge aggregation of articles that have appeared in the paper, including a page on CDOs. What you won't find is what I'd like to see as well: the original uber-explainer—call it the baseline copy—and then the current, updated version so you can see what's changed. Alternatively, it might be nice to see them mashed together, with the changes highlighted using colors for additions and strike-throughs for deletions. (You also won't find, inexplicably and inexcusably, an element that would vastly improve a Times Topics page: links to journalism other than the newspaper's own stories.)

The average reader would probably go to the updated Big Topic story, starting and ending there for the moment. Then, when new journalism appeared about CDOs, he or she would have more useful background to understand the nuances.

Again, as noted above, this idea isn't all that new. In fact, wire services understood it a long time ago. The Associated Press and others have long used what's called the "write-through"—adding new information to breaking news and telling editors what's new in the story. Now, by adapting this to the Web, we can tell everyone.

Updating Updates and Corrections

Not only can we tell people what's new, but we can (and should) tell them what we've gotten wrong. I've noted in earlier chapters that a key part of transparency is telling our audiences about our mistakes and fixing them quickly—but that's not all we can or should do.

As we update our baseline stories (and anything else we publish), we can *show* our audience what's changed. Scott Rosenberg, author of several books about the Internet, is among several people to suggest that a software industry technique called "versioning" become a normal part of journalism.

Scott, a friend who has worked with me on several projects, started pushing this after Politico. comexcised a highly relevant tidbit from a story and then pretended that what it had removed—an admission of how insider journalism, Politico's stock in trade, actually works—wasn't important in the first place. He wrote:

> Any news organization that strives to present a version of reality to its readers or users must come to grips with the fact that reality is always changing. Print publications have always taken daily, weekly or monthly snapshots of that reality, and everyone understands the relationship between the publication date and the information published under it. Radio and TV offer a closer-to-live reflection of the ever-changing news reality, but until the Web's arrival their content was so fleeting that the new update pretty much obliterated the old version of any story.
>
> The Web changes all of this. It is both up-to-the-minute and timeless—ephemeral and archival. This offers newsrooms a fundamentally different opportunity for presenting timely story updates while honoring and preserving the record of previous versions. Sadly, not a single news organization I'm aware of has yet taken advantage of this opportunity.

The nearly absurd irony is that journalism organizations already do this—internally. Every editing system of any sophistication saves copies of previous versions of articles or other content. What none of them do, save Wikipedia, is to give the audience access to all previous versions. Like Scott Rosenberg, I consider this a no-brainer that nevertheless will take years to catch on, if it ever does.

If you have a WordPress blog or a Drupal site, or have created a wiki using the standard MediaWiki software, you're in luck. There are plug-ins (or modules, which are essentially the same thing) for WordPress and Drupal that will expose your changes the way Wikipedia does.

What none of these do, however, is give you the best kind of view into what's changed. If you use Microsoft Word and collaborate on documents, you've already seen the "Track Changes" feature that gives you a great view into what's changed (and who's changed it, in collaborative settings). What we need most is a Web-based Track Changes feature—and, beyond that, a way to see how documents have changed over time in a more visual way. There's a terrific opportunity here for Web developers.

A related issue is corrections, which after all are one of the ways we update our work (assuming we're honest about correcting our mistakes). In Chapter 8, when I said what I would do if I ran a news organization, I wrote about creating a service to notify online readers, should they choose to sign up for it, of errors we've learned about in our journalism. Users of this service could choose to be notified of only errors we deemed major, or all errors, however insignificant we believed them to be.

While I'd offer this service for more general updates as well, it strikes me as especially critical for mistakes. By implementing such a system, we could help prevent new viewers from seeing incorrect information. We could also do our best to ensure that people who read incorrect information will learn that it was wrong—and that we cared enough to fix our errors.

Jack Shafer, Slate.com's media writer, has been offering this service in a technically crude way for some time. At the bottom of his column you'll find this offer:

> Track my errors: This hand-built RSS feed will ring every time Slate runs a "Press Box" correction. For e-mail notification of errors in this specific column, type the word Harman in the subject head of an e-mail message, and send it to slate.pressbox@gmail.com.

See? This isn't all that difficult!

Think Tank

Corporate R&D operations try to pick winners while making relatively "safe" bets. This is the inverse.

Imagine a small team of, for lack of a better word, "connectors." They'll identify interesting ideas, technologies and techniques—business models as well as editorial innovations. Then they'll connect these projects with people who can help make them part of tomorrow's journalistic ecosystem.

Where will these projects come from? Everywhere: universities, corporate labs, open-source repositories, startups, basements, you and me.

Part of this is about connecting dots. I take it for granted—based on my own experiences and observations over three decades—that a large percentage of those journalistically valuable ideas, technologies and techniques will come from projects whose creators have no journalistic intent. The experiments are taking place inside and outside of companies, inside and outside the news industry (mostly outside), in Silicon Valley and out in the larger world.

Who can help the connectors spread innovation into the larger ecosystem? Among others:

- Traditional news organizations. This isn't to suggest they should not invest in some internal R&D (though most do little, if any). However, I would suggest that they devote a bigger part of that spending to buy or license other people's innovations.

- Investors outside the journalism business. Angel investors and venture capitalists think "entertainment" when they think about media. They may be willing to place some of their high-risk, high-reward bets on projects that meet community information needs if they can be persuaded that they are based on serious business models.

- Non-media enterprises. More and more corporations and non-profits of all stripes are creating media. If they can help support innovations that also serve journalistic purposes, everyone wins. If they can be persuaded of the value of applying journalistic principles to what they produce, so much the better.

- Foundations. Some are spending a great deal of money now on new projects, but they'd get even more leverage by supporting the connectors.

- Individual (or small-team) media creators who can invest only their time. An essential part of the connectors' role would be to identify open-source and other such projects that regular folks or small teams can put to good community-information use.

What distinguishes the connectors?

First, they'll understand technology at a reasonably deep level. It's not necessary to be a programmer, but it's vital to know how to a) ask the right questions of the right people, b) recognize cool technology when they see it, and c) have a sound sense of the difference between cool and useful.

Second, they'll need to appreciate journalism's essential role in society, and how the craft is changing. This means understanding fundamental principles, of course, but also the need to turn journalism from the lecture mode of the past to the conversational mode it needs to become.

Third, they'll need a broad array of contacts in the technology, business, education, philanthropic, investor and other sectors—and the ability to have intelligent conversations with any of them.

Finally, they'll need to be evangelists, selling all these people not just on the need to combine great ideas with journalism, but also the need to take risks in new areas.

The catalyzing opportunities here are fairly amazing, if we pull this off. It'll require a team effort in the end, but it's definitely worth the effort—because the payoff for journalism could easily dwarf the investment.

Trust, Reputation and More

In an era where we have nearly unlimited amounts of information at our fingertips, one of the key issues is how to separate the good from the bad, the reliable from the unreliable, the trustworthy from the untrustworthy, the useful from the irrelevant. Unless we get this right, the emerging diverse media ecosystem won't work well, if at all.

I've long believed that we'll need to find ways to combine popularity—a valuable metric in itself—with reputation. This sounds easier than it is, because evaluating reputation is enormously complex. But whoever gets this right is going to be a huge winner in the marketplace.

What do we mean by reputation? In this context, many things. If someone points to a news article, for example, we have to consider reputation at many levels. Among these:

- What "media outlet"—traditional, blog, whatever—is behind the article? If it's *The Economist*, the reputation starts at a high level. If it's Joe's Blog, and I have no idea who Joe is or what he has been doing for the past few years, the reputation starts (much) lower.

- What is the reputation of the writer/video-maker/etc.? I generally give a high rating to *New York Times* reporters, but reputation can vary within organizations: I can name a few *Times* reporters who've wrecked their credibility with me over the past few years.

I gave you more detailed exploration of techniques for gauging trustworthiness and reputation in Chapter 3. Detached measurement of reputation is incredibly hard, though, and currently the tools for measuring are at best crude.

In a world of emerging digital tools, however, there are glimmerings of hope. I've been begging people at eBay for years—to no avail—to make people's reputations as buyers and sellers portable. By that I mean people should be allowed to create a badge of some kind, with some real data behind it, that they can post on their own work, with the data made available in a granular way.

Of course, your eBay reputation is not an exact proxy for your general trustworthiness, as a person or as an information creator. For one thing, we know that people are constantly gaming eBay's system. For another, how you behave in buying and selling goods online doesn't necessarily predict how you'll behave in other situations. Still, it may be a useful thing to know.

Your Karma at Slashdot is another useful metric. So are the individual users' contributions in the collaborative filtering at the Digg and Reddit websites for rating the news. Useful, but clearly not sufficient by themselves to let you make big decisions about someone's overall integrity.

Combine a bunch of reputation systems, though, and you're getting somewhere—and a world of interactive data suggest at least the possibility of finding a way to blend various measures into something that is more useful than what we have today.

Fix the Pulitzers

The people who run the Pulitzer Prizes, undoubtedly America's premier journalism awards, took useful steps into the modern age in 2008 and 2009, mainly by welcoming online-only entries. They opened the awards to people like Josh Marshall at Talking Points Memo, among many others who'd been excluded in the past due to an anachronistic system that had admitted only print entries. We should celebrate that progress.

But the new rules didn't begin to address the more fundamental issues about how journalism is changing—and they raised the question of whether journalism prizes should exist in the first place.

Let's answer the second question first. In general, journalism prizes should not exist. No other profession (or craft) gives itself as many awards as journalism. Anyone with a byline or identifiable broadcasting face or voice almost can't help winning something just by staying around long enough. Worse, many of the awards are sponsored by the people journalists cover, and some of those come with cash awards, raising all kinds of issues about integrity.

When I'm the czar of all journalism, I'll do away with almost every journalism prize. Since neither will happen, I suggest that we make the very top awards more meaningful for the digital era. Here's some of what I said to the Pulitzer Prize Board when it asked me to answer some questions and offer my own suggestions about how the prizes should recognize changes in technology and journalistic practices:

Q: In creating the Prizes, Joseph Pulitzer wanted to "elevate" the profession of journalism. In his era, better journalism meant better newspapers. How could we further his goal today, given the makeup of news media and their challenges?

A: Become the top prizes for journalism of any kind. Do away entirely with the distinction between newspapers and other media. There's no real alternative.

Q: Should the nature of the "newspaper" be redefined as multimedia journalism grows and practices change? If so, how? For example, should we include entirely online newspapers? And what should we do with things like videography and its impact on visual journalism?

A: You can't define your way out of this dilemma, except in one sense. You can define what you mean by "great journalism," and what you mean by "elevating the craft." Beyond that, everything should be fair game.

Q: Should we re-examine and possibly revise the Prizes' journalism categories? If so, how? For example, should we have a separate category for large multimedia packages? Should we reconsider the idea of circulation size as a basis for category definition—at least in some cases?

A: I'd revise the categories in some fairly dramatic ways, but I would not make separate categories for media formats, for the reasons I mentioned above.

I would, however, add several areas where the Pulitzers could elevate journalism in a big way. Here are just three:

1. The digital space has many characteristics, but one is that the journalism we create doesn't disappear into birdcages or pay-per-view databases. Stories and projects can accrete influence, and be timely long beyond the traditional periods. This is especially important when we recognize that the manufacturing process of journalism—create something and send it out, period—becomes obsolete in due course. Some ideas that take this into account:

> a. We'd all benefit from a prize celebrating relentless journalism over time that led to long-term solutions of big problems; this would require a rule change to look back more than 12 months.
>
> b. Along those lines, why not recognize reporting that was ahead of its time? Whenever a major national or international crisis becomes obvious, such as the current credit and housing meltdowns, we can always look back and find examples of prescient journalism that was essentially ignored at the time. If you made that single addition to the prizes, you'd be making a huge advance.
>
> c. And what about journalism that has evolved? I'm working on a book that will live and evolve mostly online, and I guarantee it'll be vastly better in five years than it will be the day it's officially published for the first time. I can show you things that have been updated over time, and which now are as good as journalism can be, even though they were, early on, shadows of what they've become.

2. I'd also find ways to recognize more of the finest work by small entities that do brilliant coverage of small communities of geography or interest. Beat reporting doesn't fully cover what I'm talking about here, but it's the closest you have now. (I'm not talking about separate prizes for big and little organizations, however.)

3. I'd create a prize for innovation in journalism, recognizing an advance by someone who used the collision of media and technology to create something new and valuable to the craft.

Put all of this out for public comment, by the way. You'll be amazed at the great ideas others will have.

Q: Should we re-evaluate the kind of journalism we honor and the entries we encourage? For example, do we sometimes foster journalism projects and packages that lack relevance to everyday lives?

A: Of course you do, but that's the nature of giving prizes. I don't have a great antidote for the bigness impulse. I would try to tweak the rules and judging to favor things that genuinely lead to a better world. I don't have any obvious ways to achieve this, of course....

Q: Should the Board itself be changed? Should we alter the mix of journalists and academics? Should we expand the Board's total size? (The Board now has 17 voting members, 4 of whom can be non-journalists. The dean of the journalism school and the Pulitzer administrator are non-voting members of the Board.)

A: Yes, change the board, in significant ways if you adopt any of the ideas I've suggested. (It seems large enough now.) The current board members are superb representatives of the 20th-century manufactured-newspaper model of journalism, and people of that stature and accomplishment should remain part of the mix. But I'd include some very different kinds of folks, who may have a wider vision of the craft.

Get Policy Right

As the business model of journalism has fractured, some big news organizations, their corporate parents and a host of well-meaning observers have latched onto an alarming, anti-capitalistic notion: government (read: taxpayer) help. In 2009 and 2010, the Federal Trade Commission held several workshops entitled "How Will Journalism Survive the Internet Age?," whose stated purpose was "to explore how the Internet has affected journalism."

This seemed to indicate that the nation's scam artists, monopolists and market-riggers had all gone into hibernation, during the worst economic crisis since the Great Depression. How else could the FTC have the breathing room it needs to intercede in an arena where its role is, at best, unclear?

The FTC justified its intervention in a Federal Register Notice that observed, in a promising start, that the Internet has created unparalleled possibilities. The commission could have stopped there, and not bothered to hold the workshop. It could have recognized that we're in the early days of a transition from one set of business models (most of which have not been very competitive) to an emerging, hyper-competitive sphere.

But the commission staff and many speakers found much to fret about, spurred in large part by the newspaper industry's incessant whining. (Could it also have been influenced by the fact that the FTC chairman is <u>married</u> to a *Washington Post* opinion writer? No, this obviously had absolutely no bearing on anything.) Chief among the threats was the erosion of the advertising-based business model.

The FTC notice, quoting several economists, asserted bizarrely that "public affairs reporting may indeed be particularly subject to market failure."

Market failure? What about the market failure—which, as far as I can tell, never got any attention from a succession of FTC people during the past half-century—that resulted in the the media monopolies and oligopolies that dominated that period? Their public affairs journalism was, for the most part, a modest spinoff of the extortionate advertising prices they charged when they had near-absolute market power to charge anything they wished. Only when there's real competition, it seems, does the FTC get interested.

We do not need government subsidies aimed specifically at journalism. That's not to say taxpayers should stay entirely clear of Internet deployment; in fact, a policy leading to widespread, open broadband access for all Americans is the single place where government intervention in media makes sense, with free speech implications as well as financial ones.

As noted earlier in this volume, we should remember the indirect subsidies of low postal rates for print publications, giveaways of publicly owned airwaves (spectrum) to broadcasters, the odious "Newspaper Preservation Act" granting partial antitrust immunity to community newspapers, and a variety of other special favors the news business has received over the years. Some of those were targeted directly at news organizations; others were more general and defensible.

On the table now are such fixes as changing the copyright laws to make life more difficult for online aggregators, changing antitrust laws to give journalism-related businesses even more antitrust immunity, direct subsidies and more. All are terrible ideas.

There's only one subsidy that makes sense; only one that wouldn't put government meddling squarely into the practice of journalism—an inevitable result of the direct subsidies being pushed by well-meaning but misguided media thinkers. It's a subsidy for bandwidth: getting true broadband Internet access to as many people as possible, as some other nations in Europe and Asia have done.

The precedent in this case is the right one. Taxpayer-assisted infrastructure—especially the postal system and low rates for sending publications—helped create the newspaper business, and enabled a lot of other commerce. Let's bring that logic forward to the early 21st century, and enable high-speed Internet access for all Americans, and a communications infrastructure for all competitors.

Networking Market Failure Looms

As it is, we're moving toward a market failure of frightening proportions in digital networking, as the telecom industry clamps down, or threatens to, on people's ability to use Internet connections as they see fit. We're moving toward a media business consolidation that would terrify any real champion of open markets: a cable-phone duopoly.

This brings up the topic of network neutrality: the idea that carriers should not discriminate against one content provider in favor of another.

All Internet service providers already manage their network traffic in some ways, such as spam filtering. One reason I worry about new rules enforcing neutrality is the law of unintended consequences. If we allow the carriers to make special deals to favor the content of companies that pay more for special access to end users, rather than letting you and me decide what we want to use, we're heading for major trouble.

The danger signs are growing that we're moving fast toward a world where the carriers cut deals with favored providers. They've made it clear that they want to do that, and they insist they have the right. If they win this battle, you can write off the kind of robust and diverse media/journalism ecosystem we've been discussing in this book—because upstarts will tend to be frozen out by the mega-players.

This is why it was so worrisome when Google and Verizon, the huge phone and Internet company, announced in August 2010 some principles about network access that could, if enacted, be the end of any hope of network neutrality.

They paid lip service to net neutrality, but then offered several caveats. Neutrality would apply only to the "wireline" portion of the Internet, such as DSL and cable connections, and only to what we have now. Their proposal would, they said, promote the expansion of new services that would go beyond anything we have today. Supposedly, these new services could not be designed to be end runs around net neutrality; they would have to be genuinely new.

What's the problem, then? It's this: We cannot trust Verizon or other carriers, or Google for that matter, to follow through in ways that are truly in the interest of the kind of open networks the nation needs.

If Google CEO Eric Schmidt was telling the truth when he said his company's overwhelming focus will remain on the public Internet—for example, promising that YouTube will remain there—that's great. I have no reason to disbelieve him, and Google's track record to date is strong on this issue. But plans change, managements change, and corporate strategies change.

Meanwhile, Google and Verizon went backwards in a big way, arguing that data services provided by mobile-phone companies shouldn't be subject to neutrality rules, given the constrained bandwidth on current mobile networks. As Susan Crawford, professor at Cardozo Law School of Yeshiva University in New York and an expert on all things Internet, explains: "That's a huge hole, given the growing popularity of wireless services and the recent suggestion by the [FCC] that we may not have a competitive wireless marketplace."

For Verizon's part, the acceptance of what sounded like fairly serious neutrality rules on current wire-line networks was welcome. But I see the rest as a Trojan Horse. Verizon and other carriers have every incentive, based on their legacies, to push network upgrade investments into the parallel Internet, not the public one.

With one exception, the carriers have all but abandoned their push to bring to the U.S. the kind of wired-line bandwidth that other nations— Japan, South Korea, France and Sweden come immediately to mind—enjoy. Verizon has all but stopped building out its fast fiber-optic network to homes, leaving Comcast as the provider that is most ardently boosting connection speeds via its cable lines. (Even Comcast's fast speeds are nothing special next to what carriers in those other nations have provided, not to mention initiatives elsewhere as the U.S. falls further behind.)

So when Verizon CEO Ivan Seidenberg said "We have to be flexible," my immediate thought was "Uh-oh."

The right way forward is to have sufficient bandwidth that all of us, citizens and corporations alike, can do pretty much anything we choose using public networks—a true broadband infrastructure is the basis for all communications.

Instead, the game is on by powerful corporations to create a parallel Internet that's just another version of television. Let's hope they won't get away with it.

Reward Systems

A fierce and fascinating debate broke out over the cover photo on *Time* magazine's April 27, 2009, print edition. *Time* paid a pittance for the picture of a glass jar semi-filled with coins, for a story on Americans' newly frugal ways in the wake of the financial meltdown. The amount was much less than what big magazines normally pay for cover art, and that made a lot of professional photographers furious.

They should get over it. But they and their gifted-amateur and part-timer peers—especially the ones capturing breaking news events—should start agitating for some better marketplaces than the ones available today. As I noted in Chapter 4, I'm not a fan of a system that tells people they should be contributing their work to profitable corporations for nothing more than a pat on the back.

The freelance system of the past was inefficient. If you had a great picture, your options were limited. But as the *Time* photo suggests, the marketplace in the Internet era has changed irrevocably. Someone with a camera (probably part of a phone) almost always will be in a position to capture relevant still photos and/or, increasingly, videos of newsworthy events. We'll have *more* valuable pictures, not less, and production values will take second place to authenticity and timeliness.

This is also becoming more and more the case for what journalists call "feature photography." As anyone who spends any serious time on Flickr already knows, amateur photographers are doing incredible work. Few of them can match the consistent quality of what the pros do, but they don't have to. Every one of us is capable of capturing one supremely memorable image. Whatever you're looking for, you can find it on Flickr or other photo sites, including the stock-photos service where Robert Lam listed the picture that ended up on *Time*'s cover. According to a conversation thread on the Model Mayhem photo community site, which includes some strenuous objections from pro photographers, Time paid Lam $30 for the photo.

It does strike me as absurd that a huge magazine with huge circulation can get an image like Lam's for so little money. But that was his choice, and it was *Time*'s choice to take advantage of the low price he was asking.

Just as some people gladly take the *New York Times*'s absurdly low pay when their freelance articles make it into the paper's news and op-ed pages, some photographers gladly sell their work for peanuts to *Time*. They have their own reasons, which can range from getting valuable exposure—so they can (try to) charge more for subsequent work—to not needing the higher rates that staffers and more famous people can demand.

This gets trickier, it seems to me, when it comes to breaking news, where news organizations derive enormous benefits from having the right image or video at the right time, and too frequently get it for less than peanuts. Indeed, practically every news organization now invites its audience to submit pictures and videos, in return for which the submitters typically get zip.

Which is why we need a more robust marketplace than any I've seen so far—namely, a real-time auction system.

How would a real-time auction system work? The flow, I'd imagine, would go like this: Photographer captures breaking news event on video or audio, and posts the work to the auction site. Potential buyers, especially media companies, get to see watermarked thumbnails and then start bidding. A time limit is enforced in each case. The winning bid goes to the photographer, minus a cut to the auction service.

The premium, then, would be on timeliness and authenticity. One or two images/videos would be likely to command relatively high prices, and everything else would be worth considerably less.

Eventually, someone will do this kind of business—which could also be useful for eyewitness text accounts of events. For the sake of the citizen journalists who are not getting what they deserve for their work, I hope it's sooner rather than later.

For print, an auction system is also needed, but the timeliness is less critical. A British startup is planning, as I write this, to launch a service called "Newsrupt," aimed more at editors than reporters. I hope it's the first of many such ventures.

Identity, Accountability

I said earlier that I strongly encourage people to use their real names in online conversations. But I do recognize the need for anonymity in certain situations, and I would never support the too-frequent calls for its outright banning.

My reason for preferring real names is accountability. The quality and trustworthiness of what we say and do is enhanced by our willingness to be accountable.

There are middle grounds between absolute name verification and anonymity. Online, we can use pseudonyms—made-up names—that are attached to a single e-mail address. Many online comment systems insist on registration using this method.

After all, who are you? Actually, you are many people, at least in the sense of how you deal with others in your life. You show one part of yourself to your family. You show another to your colleagues at work. And you show still another to your friends outside of home and work.

The systems for pseudonymity are still crude, though, and subject to gaming by spammers and others who want to pollute our experiences. They need to improve.

We also need to create online identities for commercial purposes— identities that guarantee merchants that we can pay but that shield all other information from being sucked into their computers. The technology exists to make this possible, but it hasn't been put into the marketplace in any consistent or robust way.

Media Literacy

I discussed this in the previous chapter, but I'll make the pitch again: We need, in America and the world, to ensure that children grow up with the kinds of media skills they mostly don't have today.

Then we need to make those skills part of a general lifelong learning process.

The principles I outlined in Chapter 2 are a good place to start. But we should not stop with helping people become better consumers; it's essential, as I've said repeatedly in this book, to focus on the creation side of the equation, too.

Those skills should add up to something larger: critical thinking. The way to have an informed citizenry is by having citizens who think for themselves.

Continue the Conversation

We've reached the end of this book, apart from the epilogue. But we're nowhere near the end of the conversation we all need to have, and continue, about our media future.

I hope you'll stop by Mediactive.com. Tell us about resources you've discovered that will help us all, and join the conversations we're having there about these issues.

More importantly, have these conversations where you live. I hope what you've read here will spark a few of them.

Epilogue, and Thanks

Whatever medium you're using to read these words, it's not part of the traditional publishing industry. Some of the folks in that business aren't thrilled with one of the ways I try to spread my ideas. My publisher is me, with the help of a company called Lulu, an enterprise that understands the changes the publishing world.

Some background: In late 2009, when I started serious work on the book part of this project, I was under contract to the publisher that brought out *We the Media* a few years ago. We parted company early in 2010, at which point my literary agent—the beyond-terrific David Miller of the Garamond Agency—started looking for a new publisher.

David told me at the outset that the potential field would be limited because I had a non-negotiable requirement: The book had to be published under a Creative Commons license, as *We the Media* had been, and publishers comfortable with Creative Commons (like my former publisher) are rare. For both books the Creative Commons license says, essentially, that anyone can make copies of the work for non-commercial use, and that if they create derivative works—also only for non-commercial purposes—those works must be made available a) with credit to me and b) under the same license.

The principle is simple: While I want my writing to get the widest possible distribution, if anyone is going to make money on it I'd like that to be me and the people who have worked with me on it.

Almost a decade after Creative Commons was founded, and despite ample evidence that licensing copyrighted works this way doesn't harm sales, book publishers remain mostly clueless about this option, or hostile to it. As David explained to editors, the main reason I'm still getting royalty checks for *We the Media* is that the book has been available as a free download since the day it went into bookstores. This is how word about it spread. Had we not published it that way, given the indifference (at best) shown by American newspapers and magazines, the book would have sunk without a trace.

That logic persuaded no one at the major publishing houses (not that we got that far in most cases—more about that below). And to my regret, the Creative Commons roadblock forced me to turn down a deal from a publisher in New York that would have been perfect for this project had I been writing a traditional book in a traditional way, and nothing more.

But this project isn't just a book; at least, not in the way most publishers understand books, even as they dabble online. And if a principle means anything to you, you stick by it when doing so is inconvenient, not just when it's easy.

To publishers, books are items they manufacture and send out to stores in trucks, or computer files they rent to their customers, or customers of Amazon, Apple and other companies that use proprietary e-reading software to lock the work down in every possible way. In both cases, publishers crave being the gatekeepers.

Mediactive aims to be a multifaceted project. Over the next few years I hope to experiment with the ideas here in lots of media formats and styles; to keep track, you can check mediactive.com. And—this is key—I also plan to experiment with this project in the broader context of the emerging ecosystem of ideas.

That ecosystem is evolving at an accelerating rate, and the people who have had specific roles in the one that prevailed in the past—authors, literary agents, speaking agents, editors, publishers and others—are going to have to change with it. Some get this and some don't, but I'm happy to say that the people I'm working with directly today are definitely in the getting-it category.

Rejections

Editors from big publishing houses have a habit of rejecting books in what they must believe is a kind way. They say something to this effect: "It's really interesting and we like Dan a bunch, and while it isn't for us we're sure it'll find a great home with someone else."

Please, folks. Any competent author would prefer this: "We didn't like it, and here's why…." Honest criticism is more helpful.

One reason several editors did offer was a bit surprising. One editor wrote, echoing several others, "The main problem that people had was that they felt that they knew much of the information that Dan was trying to get across…."

Wow. You mean that people who read and publish books for a living already know the value of deep and thoughtful media use? Right. But one of the major motivations for this project is the ample evidence that way too many other people don't know this.

Several editors liked elements of what I was doing, and wanted me to expand solely on those, to create a different book from the one I was writing. Right or wrong, I wasn't willing to abandon what I'd started.

In my days as a newspaper reporter, I learned that the only audience that really counted was my editor. This was a reality in the old world of highly concentrated media, but no more. Any serious writer needs a good editor, but the people who become your audience—and if you do it right, your collaborators—are the ones who really count.

Another "No" had the ring of truth: The publisher's publicity and marketing people "felt that the major media would avoid the book because of the criticism of their techniques." That's one reason I'm writing it....

Lulu

It was after I turned down the New York publisher's offer that I contacted Bob Young, Lulu's founder and CEO. Bob also started Red Hat, one of the first companies to prove that it was possible to make money with open-source software by providing services, and he's been an ardent supporter of ensuring that what we call "intellectual property" offers as much flexibility for creators and users as possible.

Bob had told me about Lulu several years earlier, and in that conversation he'd suggested it would be a good fit for me someday. Now, we both thought, might be the time.

He put me in touch with Daniel Wideman, Lulu's director of product management, who told me about the company's "VIP Services" for established authors making the move to this kind of publishing. Daniel said he very much liked what I was trying to accomplish in this new project, and we had several further discussions. In the end it was clear to me that this would indeed be a good fit. I'd do the writing. An editor of my choice would help make the text sing. And Lulu would handle most of the rest of the job, for a fee, including printing, binding and distribution, and some back-office tasks.

Lulu isn't the only outfit of this kind, by any means. The self-publishing business is growing quickly, in part because the old-line publishers are hunkering down these days. I like the way Lulu sees its own part in the emerging ecosystem. Doing it this way comes at a price, but it's worth it.

Incidentally, had I signed with a traditional publisher, the book would not have reached the marketplace for a year or more from the date when I signed. With a company like Lulu, you wrap up the project and you're off to the races. In a fast-moving area like media, that's a huge benefit to foregoing the standard route.

Version 1.0

Think of what you're reading as Mediactive 1.0, the first major release in what I expect to be a work that changes with its times. A year from now, I hope to launch Mediactive 2.0 in print– a fully updated book that takes into account what I've learned in the months since publishing the first edition.

I very much hope that you will be part of the updating process. Please tell me what I've gotten wrong and what I've missed.

I'll be updating the Mediactive website more regularly. You'll be able to find previous versions of this book's chapters, along with the current versions. We're still working out the best way to help people who may have cited a version that's since been revised. This is one of the important issues in publishing in this new century: What is the baseline, anyway, when we can keep fixing and improving?

Acknowledgments

I have so many people to thank for their help on this project. They start with the people with whom I've been having a conversation about media for years. They include (alphabetically and among many others) Marko Ahtisaari, Chris Anderson, Kevin Anderson, David Ardia, Azeem Azhar, Frank Baker, John Perry Barlow, John Battelle, Sam Bayard, Emily Bell, Yochai Benkler, Guy Berger, Jim Bettinger, Krishna Bharat, Matt Biddulph, Nick Bilton, danah boyd, Stowe Boyd, James Boyle, John Bracken, Jim Brady, Jody Brannon, Dan Bricklin, John Brockman, Aaron Brown, Merrill Brown, Steve Buttry, Jason Calacanis, Chris Callahan, Serena Carpenter, Jerry Ceppos, Ying Chan, Suw Charman-Anderson, Jeff Cohen, David Cohn, CJ Cornell, Thomas Crampton, Mark Cuban, Steffi Czerny, Cory Doctorow, Steve Doig, Len Downie, Jon Dube, Esther Dyson, Renee Edelman, Richard Edelman, Werner Eggert, Charles Eisendrath, Jim Fallows, Dave Farber, Rob Faris, Seth Finkelstein, Fabrice Florin, Mei Fong, Bill Gannon, Jon Garfunkel, Bob Giles, Kristin Gilger, Steve Gillmor, Mark Glaser, Michael Goff, Ben Goldacre, Paul Grabowicz, Don Graham, Eszter Hargittai, Jay Harris, Scott Hieferman, Retha Hill, Mary Hodder, Reid Hoffman, Adrian Holovaty, Ellen Hume, Kimberley Isbell, David Isenberg, Joi Ito, Xeni Jardin, Jeff Jarvis, Alex Jones, Matt Jones, Paul Jones, Martin Jönsson, Chris Kabwato, Mitch Kapor, Scott Karp, Doug Kaye, Gary Kebbel, Dan Kennedy, David Kirkpatrick, Bruce Koon, Jonathan Krim, Andrew Leckey, Larry Lessig, Steven Levy, Harry Lewis, Andrew Lih, Caroline Little, Melissa Ludtke, Rebecca MacKinnon, Colin Maclay, Om Malik, Phil Malone, Isaac Mao, Jason Manning, John Markoff, Kevin Marks, Joshua Micah Marshall, Tim McGuire, Brock Meeks, Ari Melber, Nicco Mele, Susan Mernit, Jerry Michalski, Amanda Michel, Bill Mitchell, Allen Morgan, Walt Mossberg, Charlie Nesson, Craig Newmark, Eric Newton, Robert Niles, Allen Noren,Chris O'Brien, Oh Yeon Ho, Lise Olson, Pierre Omidyar, Steve Outing, Geneva Overholser, Ray Ozzie, Lanita Pace-Hinton, Marcia Parker, Sam Perry, Chris Pirillo, Vikki Porter, Lee Rainie, JP Rangaswami, Andrew Rasiej, Eric Rasmussen, Marcel Reichart, Howard Rheingold, Gabe Rivera, Rick Rodriguez, Jay Rosen, Scott Rosenberg, Steve Rubel, Alan Rusbridger, Richard Sambrook, Robert

Scoble, Doc Searls, Wendy Seltzer, Jake Shapiro. Frank Shaw, Jan Schaffer, Jake Shapiro. Clay Shirky, Ludwig Siegele, Dave Sifry, Micah Sifry, Craig Silverman, Lisa Sounio, Josh Stearns, Lisa Stone, Kara Swisher, Matt Thompson, Yossi Vardi, Simon Waldman, Steven Waldman, Jimmy Wales, Joan Walsh, Linton Wells, Howard Weaver, David Weinberger, Kevin Werbach, Steve Wildstrom, Ev Williams, Lisa Williams, Dave Winer, Leonard Witt, Xu Wu, Jonathan Zittrain, Ethan Zuckerman and Markos Moulitsas Zúniga. Andy Oram did an initial edit of many chapters, and was an early sounding board as I wrote. JD Lasica and Brad King read the draft and made excellent suggestions. Rachel Head copy-edited the final draft, and her tweaks and thoughts were a further improvement. I'm sure I've forgotten to mention some others; my apologies, and I trust they'll know how much I appreciate their input.

The Mediactive project was conceived at the Berkman Center for Internet & Society at Harvard University—an unparalleled pool of talent and wisdom about our new digital environment. I was a Fellow there from 2006–2009, and was asked by Persephone Miel, a Fellow who was leading a project called "Media Re:public," to write an essay for a longer document she was creating on the state of media. That essay helped me think through the principles that form the heart of this project. Persephone died in the summer of 2010, too young, and is sorely missed by all who knew her.

The book gestated at the Walter Cronkite School of Journalism & Mass Communication at Arizona State University, which has helped me see journalism in new ways as well. The school's terrific students, staff and faculty are on the front lines of journalism's evolution in this era of accelerating change, and as a university ASU is working to create a more modern model for higher education. Chris Callahan, the Cronkite School's extraordinary dean, has vision and energy that are unmatched in his field, and it's been an honor to be part of this team.

Portions of the book appeared first in my Mediactive blog and in my new column on Salon.com. The people at Salon, a pioneer in the online media world, combine a commitment to quality with a progressive spirit that inspires me.

Josh Sprague, a former graduate student of mine at Arizona State, has worked with me on the Mediactive project at various steps. His help has been invaluable.

Monitor Talent manages my speaking and consulting gigs; Chris Meyer, Mel Blake, Meghan Fennell and Jacqueline Lewis have offered terrific advice about my career and Mediactive's place in it.

Clay Shirky's insights are no secret to his growing legion of fans, of whom I'm one. He honored me by contributing the foreword to this book, and his friendship is a continuing joy.

I owe special thanks to my literary agent, David Miller, who stayed with this project even after it veered outside the traditional publishing world. David, like me, is learning about the future of media. I'm grateful for his extraordinary counsel.

The editor for this book is my longtime friend <u>Tom Stites</u>. He's a current Berkman Fellow and creator of the <u>Banyan Project</u>, which aims to bring quality journalism back to the people who may need it most: average folks who've been largely left behind. My instructions to Tom, when he took on this project, were simple: Don't let me off the hook. He hasn't, I'm glad to say, and the result is a vastly better book. Thank you, Tom.

I'm a better person thanks to Noriko Takiguchi. She makes me sane, and lights my life.

Made in the USA
Lexington, KY
04 January 2011